I only went out for a walk and finally concluded to stay out

till sundown, for going out, I found, was really going in.

—JOHN MUIR

OUTSIDE/IN

ON LOVING NATURE &
LIVING WITH PARKINSON'S

ED BIEBER

EDITED BY DALE HUSHBECK

Ragged Sky Press
Princeton, New Jersey

ALSO BY ED BIEBER
What Color Is the Wind?
A Feel Guide to the Out-of-Doors
for Parents with Young Children

Published by Ragged Sky Press
270 Griggs Drive, Princeton, NJ 08540
http://www.raggedsky.com/
All Rights Reserved
ISBN 978-1-933974-38-5
Composed in 11pt. Bembo, with
Microbrew Soft One titling
Printed on acid-free paper

THIS BOOK IS DEDICATED TO

*my wife, Jill — always there, loving and
understanding. She knows full well what it means
when they say if one person in a family has Parkinson's
the whole family has it...and she is an ardent
believer in getting Ed out-of-doors.*

*Rafael (Ray) Manaças — a gentle, kind and
competent community builder, former administrator
of the Threefold Education Center, friend and supporter
of The Nature Place for many years, and another
staunch advocate of outdoor education.*

*marking fifty years as an outdoor
educator in 2020.*

CONTENTS

. . . . P A R K **I N** S O N ' S

FOREWORD
or perhaps I should say
OUTWORD

Or outward, *because that has been my life's direction.*
Outside is where I truly belong, close by or far away,
exploring canyonlands or cracks in the sidewalk,
on cloudless summer days or starry winter nights,
in fair or foul weather, sweltering or shivering, where
I have taught and been taught every day how beautiful
our world is, how healing and generous, and where I've
learned to appreciate the universal appeal of Winnie
the Pooh's joyous exclamation: "Let's go explores!"

Nature was where I found it, growing up in North
Arlington, New Jersey, southernmost town in a county
whose northern townships were well known for
luxurious manors, spacious yards and, we assumed,
lots of money. By comparison, our little corner of
Bergen County was a blue collar hamlet of modest
homes on little lots and a few apartment complexes.
A half-hour's drive from Manhattan, ten miles
from Newark, bordered by Kearny to the south,
Lyndhurst to the north, west of the Meadowlands
and east of the ever-polluted Passaic River.

We lived on Ridge Road, the beginning of Route 17,
now a heavily traveled corridor that stretches north
into New York State, where it turns into an interstate.
My parents called it a "nice avenue," flanked by houses,
churches, banks, offices, store fronts, an ice cream shop,
taverns, a five & dime, a car wash, a public high school
and a Catholic one, vacant lots, and Holy Cross Cemetery,
which took up close to a quarter of the town's real estate.

We moved around a lot, always within
one or two blocks of Ridge Road, with too little
money, always, and too much alcohol, at times.

I remember being a scared and worried kid,
though I had a reliable cohort of friends.
My mother always exhorted my brother
and me to go outside — where the air, she said,
would be good for us — and we obliged....
We explored the alleyways, the scrubby plot
behind a neighboring apartment building,
the treed grounds of Wilson Elementary,
where we went to school. Our favorite haunts,
though, were Holy Cross Cemetery's pristine
acres — where the guards chased us for climbing
the fence — the margins of the Meadowlands,
where mounds of debris seemed to materialize
overnight; and the riverbank, where we poked
sticks at the mud-encrusted remains of creatures
whose fetid odor still molders in my memory.
There were a few parks nearby...and there was
the sky, always the wide sky. All we had to do
was look around, or look up, and nature was there.

So, while my early experiences of nature didn't
compare with those of a farmboy, or Davy Crockett,
one of my boyhood heroes, I found whatever nature
could be found in our densely populated environs.
Happily, my parents took us "down the shore"
every summer for a halcyon barefoot week
of ocean, bay and beaches. I relished every outdoor
escapade, but my bedroom wasn't full of twigs and
shells, bug collections or piles of rocks. I never owned
a magnifying glass, and I didn't delve into nature
so much as nature seemed to find me. It slowly
dawned on me that the sounding, fragrant world
of weeds, trees, birds, beasts and fickle weather wasn't really
a world apart, but my world — open, clear and close.

I reckoned this world was good, and worked pretty well,
that it was somehow important, despite most people's
not knowing too much about it. There was a sense of
belonging to it, the promise of being part of something
wholly greater than the streets of North Arlington.
I loved those streets, don't get me wrong; I played
on them every day until it was too dark to see.
We played in the mist left by the truck that trundled
through the neighborhood spraying against those
nasty "skeeters" — a pastime, knowing what I know now,
that might have cast doubt on the wisdom of Mom's
injunction to get outside, but it never occurred to us:
The world was benevolent, and the trail of fog behind
that truck was such good, giggly fun.

Entering my teens, I did well in school, suffered
the routine indignity of acne, and liked girls,
though I was not a little intimidated by them.
In the middling throng of schoolyard popularity,
with my share of cronies and obstreperous bullies,
I liked sports, but chose not to play — cowed by
the taunting of alpha-male jocks. I was fit enough
to be athletic, but my lack of competitive zeal
was apparent. Then a physical exam vetting me
for the football team in 7th grade discovered
a heart murmur, mild and no cause for alarm,
but enough to excuse me from sports without
losing face…whew! Instead I managed the
basketball team. Riding the bench at games
was a high-energy treat, but I wasn't thrilled
with schlepping equipment and sweaty uniforms,
mocked and belittled by players and (!) teachers.

Gradually, my high school status pendled between
timorous Eddie and confident Ed, with some good friends,

decent grades and an after-school job. I read a lot —
books about nature in particular. I borrowed
Lives of Famous Naturalists from the town library
repeatedly, and kept a daily weather journal
as I sat in class, taking notes on the sky out the
window to which my classmates were oddly indifferent.
Why? I wondered. How could they be so impassive?
Although the tough sitting next to me in homeroom,
who wouldn't have been caught dead talking to me
in the hallways and could crush me like a grape
if I displeased him, let me know in veiled remarks
that he thought taking sky notes was actually kinda cool.

We took aptitude tests in my freshman year that asked us
to choose: Would you rather go bowling or take a hike
in the woods? Work indoors or outside in all weathers?
My answers, needless to say, betrayed an interest
in the natural sciences and outdoor pursuits. When
we had to write a Career Paper, exploring a potential
vocation whether or not we expected to follow it,
I picked Forest Ranger. For research, I asked my cousin
Diane and her fiancé Billy to drive me to a heavily
wooded area near Ringwood. It could have been Maine
or the Pacific Northwest as far as I was concerned,
it felt so wild and remote. In a cheery log cabin
in the middle of nowhere, a patient ranger answered
my questions with kindly warmth. After I finished
that paper, I took to envisioning myself stationed
alone in a fire tower atop some rugged mountain
in a vast western preserve. Ahh, what a life.

Not for me, though, when I thought about it
seriously. I needed to be with people. At my first
real job, as a soda jerk at Nanke's, the local ice cream

parlor, I enjoyed the give-and-take of waiting
on customers and swapping tales. The shop was
closed on Wednesdays, and one of those mid-week days
in mid-summer the owner invited me to join his family
for a picnic in Harriman State Park, just over the border
in New York. I felt a tad awkward, an extra kid in tow
with a family I barely knew, but I had always gotten
a kick out of the energy and spunk of youngsters
like my boss's children. We staked out a rough-hewn
wooden table by the shore of Lake Kanawauke
for our base camp. As the kids and I ventured
farther away from the site, up and down trails
marked by paint blazes on the trees, a new world
opened for me: The park was so big! I realized
how much forest, meadow, lake and stream
there was to discover, how many paths there were
to follow, how far and wide you could walk
without seeing a single wall or window.

From that day, I became an inveterate hiker.
I threw my sneakers in a closet and bought a pair
of leather hiking boots at Morsan's (now Campmor),
then a backpack with scads of compartments to stuff
with a canteen, waterproof matches, a rain poncho,
trail maps for the tracts of Harriman north and south,
and the New York Walk Book, a nifty trail guide and
source of trivia about the natural and human history
of the parklands through which the trails meander.

At 17, while I was on the Ramapo Dunderberg Trail just
south of the Appalachian Trail on Fingerboard Mountain,
I had a moment of absolute clarity. It was a crystalline day,
early spring under a bright sun, purring with the trickle of
snowmelt and the chatter of birds. As I sat down to rest

on a rock, sip from my canteen and look slowly around,
a hush fell over everything…a wisp of grace, as I recall it
now. I was completely at home, right at that spot, in need
of nothing more. That's when the words spun through
my mind, unspooling like ticker tape: I want to share
this feeling with others — with children, especially.
That's it! I'm going to teach kids in the out-of-doors.
I didn't shout or burst into song, no fireworks went off
in my head. I didn't rush to tell the world. I. Just. Knew.

I resumed my hike. By the time I reached Fingerboard
Shelter on the AT, my mind was swimming with visions
of my future self, visiting and revisiting that place with clusters
of excited children as eager to learn about nature as I was
to share it with them. Those visions have proven real hundreds
of times over the years. I joined the Interstate Hiking Club,
soaked up what I could from the people I met there, visited
museums of nature lore, read books, hiked, and hiked, and
hiked some more. I got to know and love Harriman intimately.
Not knowing yet if my vision would unfold, or how, I majored
in botany at Rutgers University, got a master's in conservation
education at Michigan State. In the summer of 1970 I sent
resumés to nature centers all over the country until I landed
a job at Lakeside Nature Center in Spring Valley, New York —
less than 40 minutes' drive from the town where I grew up
(I could live at home 'til I got on my feet!) and a scant
12 miles as the crow flies from the site of my epiphany.

The Lakeside Nature Center was on the grounds
of a residential school for "dependent and neglected
children," most of them from New York City. Many of
these mostly Black and Hispanic children came from
unfortunate backgrounds. Part of my job as Assistant
Naturalist was to take them out and about on the school's

sprawling 150-acre campus, following and fashioning
nature trails around its farmland, woods, fields, ponds
and streams. Fittingly, for me, there was even an old
cemetery on the property (echoes of the Holy Cross
Cemetery where I used to ramble), purported to contain
the remains of George Washington's barber, of all people.
The rest of my job was to host the public school classes
that visited regularly for outdoor education programs.

Two years later, I became the center's director,
and feeling confident in that role I began to offer
the center's students and visitors off-campus day hikes
in — where else? — Harriman State Park. I had come
to know the park so well it was like conducting tours
of my backyard. And there came a day, no mistake,
as we were stopped for a water break, when I looked around
and realized: This was the very spot where I made my silent
declaration to do, someday, exactly what I was doing now.

I have been so doing ever since, in many more parks,
preserves and outposts of nature. I also came to make
more of the fact that my love of the great outdoors had
been whetted by those youthful hours amid the natural
splendors right outside the door of my family home.
Harriman was an embarrassment of riches, by comparison,
but I was convinced that people didn't actually need to
range so far to appreciate what nature has in store.
In 1976 I set out on my own, first as an independent
outdoor educator, then as the founder and director
of The Nature Place Day Camp. I have been doing
as I once imagined I could, sitting on that rock —
happily, heartily making others at home in my world.

All my life, I've been an unabashed advocate of nature,
like a street peddler hawking vials of Eddie's Outdoor Elixir:
Try it today, without delay! You'll be refreshed, less depressed,
free of judgments, braced by a world that works at its own
invigorating pace! You'll feel relaxed but exhilarated...
wholly yourself...yada, yada, yada, kumbaya.

Yesterday, though, I had a hard time convincing
myself to take a walk in Harriman State Park,
my favorite slice of nature in this entire world.
I was exhausted after nine intense weeks of running
my summer camp, Monday through Friday from
6:30 am to 9 pm, always something going on...
including the hikes I led in Harriman (I know,
what a burden, but someone had to do it).
Weekends barely sufficed for recuperation
and the making of plans for the week to come.
I'm not complaining, mind you. I love it all.
I'm reminded of Curly, the grizzled cowpoke
in *City Slickers*, who signalled the secret to a
happy life by raising the index finger of one hand:
Just do one thing, he said, to the exclusion of all else.
That's my camp...though I'm relieved it has a limited
summer run. I couldn't keep it up year 'round.

Usually, once the camp's been cleaned,
boxed up and put away until next year,
there's something of a letdown. My mind is still
dialed in to camp rhythms, but my body is spent,
I move about more slowly and take a lot of naps.
I suppose Parkinson's makes it harder to rebound;
I'm a little more achy and fatigued. Yesterday
the insomnia that comes with my malady
had me wide awake at 4 am, still bone-tired

| 1

and admittedly more than a little depressed.
Surfing the internet to pass the time, I read that
Linda Ronstadt has Parkinson's, too, and she says
she can't sing anymore, that no one with PD can sing.

I'd never heard that…I sing with kids at camp all the time.
But each Parkinson's case is unique – maybe that won't be me.
Or it is already, and the kids are either indulgent or tone-deaf?
This sour note wasn't helping my mood, so I decided
to check my bank balance, planning to pay bills later on.
Bad move. If the figure had been up *just* a bit…

That's when Charlie frisked into the room.
I'd been thinking of taking him on a hike,
but I was fumbling for excuses to put it off.
Charlie's a ten-month-old black lab/husky bundle
of vigor, doggedly clambering all over the place,
slavering, nipping and chewing without pause.
I've enjoyed hiking with my dogs in the past,
but I've been hesitant about Charlie, who may
not have outgrown his tendency to vomit
on car rides. And if I take him off the leash,
will he run away from the trail, chase every squirrel,
gobble up deer droppings, jump on other hikers,
not come when I call?

And will I have timed my medications so I
can manage the trail without freezing or stumbling?
This freezing isn't temperature-related; it's what
Parkinson's
people
can
do
when their medication wears off. Locomotion
seizes, my legs tremble, I could stagger and fall.

My upper body is still moving forward but my feet
and legs slam on the brakes. Should I bring my cane?
Nah…there's loads of walking sticks in the woods.

The sun was up by now, but the trip to Harriman
I've made countless times was inexplicably daunting.
Post-camp doldrums, bank book blues, Parkinson's
jitters, puppydog doubts…my wife watched me dithering
and gave me a push. Just go, she said, there's nothing
urgent here, the dog needs exercise, *you* need exercise,
the kids are taken care of in one place or another.
She herself was leaving for her sister's baby shower in D.C.
She made sense, which only seemed to annoy me.

Still, I started getting ready, listlessly scrounging
for my backpack and a bowl for Charlie's water.
Every step was an obstacle, none of my customary
zest for nature was rising to the fore, but we did get
to the car, finally. I drove; Charlie sat in the back seat.
I was tempted to turn back when the road to a favorite
trail was closed for repair. We took a detour, though…
as I wondered which other trail we should head for,
whether I should take my meds now or later,
if the longer ride was making Charlie queasy.

I parked close to Lake Skannatati and began
following the turquoise blazes of the Long Path.
Charlie briskly snorted at every rock, root, twig,
fern, clump of moss and splash of sunlight.
I decided to remove his leash – anxious that he might
scent a deer and chase it out of sight, never to return –
but he romped and snuffled contentedly, never
let me out of his sight for more than ten seconds,
came every time I called, politely avoided other hikers,
and proved himself an ideal companion on the trail.

I started to let nature sink in, to feel the trail
as an old friend – damaged a bit by Hurricane Sandy,
but warm and familiar – and I relaxed.

My legs functioned as they should…I was even
working up a comfortable sweat. As I stepped (nimbly,
I imagined) over rocks in the trail, across rivulets,
through forest glades where I could look up at the
cloudless sky, my whole body felt lighter, looser.
My world was working nicely, thank you…
nature was alive and well and so was I, despite
my morning of metaphorical storm damage.
I played hiding games with Charlie. I was enchanted
once more by the treasures in leaf, wood and stone
that caught my eye. I forgot about my troubles.
And the future, if I considered it at all —
well, that would be then. This was now,
and more than enough.

Confident and capable, I turned around after a mile,
and on our return I spied many things we'd missed,
including one of those walking sticks for the last stretch.
Nearing the parking lot, Charlie was hot on the scent
of our car so I figured I should reattach his leash.
A lad in the lot who hadn't yet seen the leash, or me
following, thought Charlie might be a bear cub with
his mama close behind. Greatly relieved when I came
into view holding the leash, the boy smiled sheepishly
and told me about his momentary anxiety. We stood
together under the open sky and laughed like old friends.

Step right up, folks! It's Nature. Works every time.

OUTSIDE

After weeks of waiting patiently
for the first dandelion to appear,
we opened our door on a shocking
sea of vibrant, yellow, near-stemless
lion's teeth. Crouched, or crawling
on our hands and knees, we plucked
as many as we could, laid them in
a serpentine daisy chain across the yard,
around trees, over rocks, up the steps
and along the deck of the house.

That same day, as if our lemony plunder
had triggered a call and response,
our driveway blacktop was showered
with hundreds of pink and white petals
from our cherry tree, perfectly spaced
each from the other (how, I wondered,
by whom, by what patient hand?).
I got on my hands and knees again,
puffed at the petals and watched them
billow away and settle in fragile wisps
of ticklish, haphazard pastel. I blew
time and again, from one side, then
another. My neighbor, if he happened
to be watching, must have wondered
why I didn't use a leaf blower. Or
he might have considered joining me.

| 7

Once, I thought it was enough to be clever.
I led them into woods and wilds and told them
where to step or stop, when to look or listen.
I expected they would pay rapt attention
to my artful anecdotes about plants, animals,
geology, history, ecology. I was the consummate
guide, sure of the terrain with or without a map,
spouting facts and canny patter, the nature savant.
Smell this leaf, I said, or hear the hammering woodpecker.

I came to understand I'd been a bad example.
I'd brought the lesson out of doors, freed from walls
and ceilings, but never dropped my mantle of authority,
didactic beside the oak tree instead of the blackboard,
the wise preceptor of truths and facts, as my charges
followed dutifully, or pretended to.

What happened to the verve that first drew me to nature –
the fun and adventure, discoveries waiting to be made,
the joy, the hands-on engagement, the wonder of it all?
Why was I screening these children from the opportunity
to sharpen all their senses, learn for themselves, light upon
something utterly new, different from what anyone
else, myself included, had ever seen or heard?

I have since learned to do more by doing much less.
By just heading out the door, my job is close to fully done.
I start exploring wordlessly, without expectations.
I share my delight and surprise, talk to the trees,
press my hand to them, or my ear, and the pleasure
I take in all of it is all the children need to be informed
…and happily so. I may lead at first, or at random, but
more often than not I drop the reins and hold my tongue.

Nature is the master here: boundless, unpredictable,
full of astonishments. The children come next. I follow.

The snow has been crusted with ice for days. Small
children might tread without breaking the surface,
but most of us chunk through, sinking into the understory
of soft snow, six inches or more of it under the carapace.
As each step leaves behind clumps of ice and snow,
I can't resist wanting to rearrange them, fashioning
hearts, gnome homes, ziggurats…or a snaking
track that resembles the scaly tail of a dragon.

Of course, I try first to walk over unbroken stretches
as gingerly as possible, picturing my weight spread
out like a waterbug skating the surface of a pond.
I surmise I should sink less often then, my body
and disbelief suspended by the sway of imagination.
Mind over matter? Have I become so much
like a child again that my bulk has followed suit?
No matter…that child has been seduced by dragon tails.

As near as the smallest backyard,
as far away as the Amazon rainforest,
and in all the in-betweens, the weeds
of nature's irrepressible force are there,
between buildings and roads, tunnels
and bridges, endlessly sprouting,
puncturing streets and sidewalks,
cracking the macadam of parking lots,
bursting, time and again, through
asphalt and stone-solid concrete.

To quote Jon Kabat-Zinn,
wherever you go, there you are.
But you're not alone. None of us is, ever.
Nature is always there, all the time.
You and nature are never removed
from one another, never estranged.

In the midst of condominiums,
on school grounds or vacant lots,
overlooked in a stand of trees
at the end of the block, or in
greenways, vest pocket parks,
rights of way for pipes or poles,
on every side of where you live.
In that narrow patch of grass
separating sidewalk and curb.
In the very air you breathe.

There is more than you realize
in the half-light behind your garage
or the sunlit crack in the sidewalk,
in the scents that perfume the air
at the beach, in a miasmic swamp,
in fecund wilderness or infertile desert,
in national parks or town square memorials.

You get this, of course.
But don't just get it – get up,
and get out. Get the everywhere
of nature under your fingernails,
into your lungs, on the tip
of your tongue, at the front
of your mind, in the beat
of your heart.

Yesterday morning's rain was turning
to ice the second it hit the ground –
or touched anything, for that matter,
auguring accidents and cancellations.
I stayed inside all day for a change, playing it safe.

When I ventured out again today,
I was surprised to see rocks and boulders
still wholly enrobed in ice, like Easter eggs
dipped in a glacial balm, lustrous and glistening.
I bent down to examine them slowly, transfixed,
tracing their contours with numbing fingers.

Nature's art reveals itself subtly, quietly,
in unexpected spells whose swift surprise
– though it may last no longer than a wintry
moment, an hour or a shadowed morning –
has lovely, lingering charms and powers.
I wondered how long these gelid gems would stay
suspended in their watery shells. I'm glad
I was there to greet them, to be caught up
in their frozen while, before I slipped away.

I've worked with thousands of children,
of all ages and backgrounds, from good
schools and bad, from cities, suburbs and
rural hamlets, facing special needs or emotional
hurdles, in all seasons, for months at a time
or no more than a few golden hours.

In my twenties I worked with neglected kids,
tough customers, racially diverse, city-bred.
I took them for day hikes in Harriman Park,
five days of canoeing in the Adirondacks or,
once, on a seven-week, cross-country camping trip.
Their home lives were completely different
from anything I'd ever known, as a white man
brought up and educated in comparatively
privileged circumstances. They were just kids,
glad for the chance to be in the fresh air, grateful
for cerulean days with no clouds of suspicion.

There have been many get-out-into-nature books
published lately…based, perhaps, on rosy memories
of childhoods when the authors played freely, roamed,
explored, built forts, tucked frogs in their pockets,
and wouldn't return home until the sun had set.
When they lived and breathed the march of seasons fully.
They recall lives that seem to have been much better
than those of so many children today. Today's children
often miss out on all of that. How sad for the children.
We need to do more for the children.

I've been finding inspiration
in the stumps of fallen trees,
their jagged edges jutting up
like cityscapes, or cypress knees.

I paint them in with doors and windows,
refinishing these timber tines,
these silhouettes of sylvan wrack,
as metropolitan skylines.

When winter comes my woodsy muse
can slip into a dormant mode.
I'll need to seek out other stumps
when the weather's not so cold.

Still, nature's wintry art surprises
as I cross a barren parking lot.
Here and there, along my way,
I'm caught by unexpected spots.

Glancing down to step with care,
not thinking about errant treasure,
I'm struck by nature's odd designs,
her intricacies beyond measure.

The incidental interplay
of salt and snow and raking light
tints the macadam over and over,
day by day – no, that's not right –

more like a watercolor canvas,
this asphalt palimpsest renews
constantly, as every moment
shimmers with quicksilver hues.

Now! See that? No, wait, it's gone…
these subtle, swift ephemera
tempt me time and again to think
I should have brought my camera.

Spellbound in a parking lot? That's strange,
my wife jests, though she knows
the extra- in the ordinary
is a magic realm that comes
and goes.

There's nothing like the greasy scent
of insect repellant in the morning!
I know that smell. The chemical fetor
of someone, or their near and dear,
seeking immunity from bites and rashes.
Children, their eyes squeezed tightly shut,
wait for their dosing, front and back,
head to toe, every quarter sprayed
by a careful, caring parent or teacher.

Before long they're fully shrouded,
before anyone can even be sure a spritz
is needed. Like adding salt and pepper
before you've tasted your food.
It's part of our habitual buffering
from the world of nature, fueled
by misgivings that "out there'"
is somehow alien, possibly dangerous.

But nature is not foreign to me.
It does not visit from some distant,
unknown, viral place, nor do I
need to travel far to find it.
It's where I've been all along,
where I already spend my time.
Nothing exotic or fraught with
pestilence, no latent threats
of contamination. If you don't
live in a swamp, or a tropical
rainforest, join me. Stick your toe
in the water, turn your face
to the sun, take a good look around.
DEET is *optional*.

...your soul grows clear and quiet
in nature's limpid hush, in her
unhurried times and spaces
where marvels blossom wild and free,
a sphere of calm and constant comfort.
Stay a wondering while and breathe.

...worries cease to burden you.
Nature doesn't fret or fluster,
nor should you, when there's so much
to take in, look for and discover,
devoid of petty cares and woes.

... thirsting for fulfillment wanes.
The thought that once you do this,
or have that, you will magically thrive
is all rank absurdity. Nature has no
blind ambition, no sublime bourn
it must achieve. It continues, unabated,
untrammeled by some aching need.

...all things unfold as they should.
We breathe, as do the leaves and trees.
Spring follows winter, bugs eat bugs,
the sun arcs east to west each day,
the world is as it's meant to be,
there's no call to force or shape it.

...outdoors, we feel a balance,
connected overall to all.
Every presence has its purpose.
A pretty sweet set-up. Everything works.
Plants and planets. Snails and gulls.
Soils and seas. Everything!
Amazing. How sweet the sound.

We began in 1976, responding in part
to the women's groups we had heard
or read about, getting together to talk
about what it means to be a *man*,
how we might support each other,
not sure of our purpose or intentions –
Therapy? Play? Making new friends?
Most of us admitted to having few
"real" friends, only acquaintances.
We settled on an opportunity to gather,
without the general manly pretexts of
politics, business, war, sports…drinking.
Well, maybe a little of such things,
but more substance than palaver.

Old or young(ish), married or not, with
or without children, white collar or blue –
we tried meeting weekly for a few months
before settling into an uneven monthly rhythm.
We meet at our homes, in bowling alleys,
for dinners, movies, concerts and plays.
Hiking through woods under a full
moon. No howling.

Despite how much we enjoy the outdoors,
we've come to agree winter outings take
a toll on our aging frames, and we're so
preoccupied with our exertions, watching
our steps, falling behind, catching up,
cracking wise, talking about women (uh-huh,
still lots of that), snacking on trail mix and
trivia, we wind up overlooking the woods.
"What business have I in the woods," wrote Thoreau,
"if I am thinking of something outside the woods?"

Sapped by the hectic day-to-day, we need
to recharge our batteries, leave behind
what weighs on our spirits, rise in the present.
We are not hardy, sinewed, muscular men,
born for tracking wilderness, who might
live for weeks in the hinterlands with nothing
but the clothes on our backs and a penknife.
Picture instead a teacher, a social worker, an architect,
a small business owner, a court reporter, a landlord,
a contractor, a retiree. Not Casper Milquetoast
exactly, but certainly not Daniel Boone.
Leaders at times, maybe, but more likely followers,
more accidental bushwhackers than trailblazers.
Treading passages outside and inside, we coalesce
as our paths entwine in sunlight and friendship,
sons of fathers who may have taught by example
the debatable virtues of sarcasm, of taking
relationships for granted, of hiding their feelings,
of drinking to numb, recuse or forget.

Mary Oliver offers *Instructions for living a life*:
Pay attention. Be astonished. Tell about it.
We're not too proud to take her advice.
We would simply add, to begin with: Get Out.
We get out of the house, get out of our own way,
get out with others who've got getting out
on their minds. We are made bold to tell others:
Get out of your rut, and get into life. That's the
main reason why, years later, we keep on meeting.

This mid-September has had cool nights,
blue-sky days puffed with fair-weather clouds,
the midday sun shedding the kind of gentle
warmth that makes you yawn with pleasure.
The same sun in midsummer would send you,
sweltering, in search of shade. Not today.

I had promised to take Nathaniel and two
of his friends fishing, where the Ramapo River
banks along the western fringe of Harriman Park.
We parked in a hidden lot we had often bypassed
on our way to the park's hiking trails, next to
a broad stretch of river with plenty of room
to cast your line. Recent lack of rain had left
the water nearly pond-still. Across the stream,
the trees, shrubs, wetlands and darting dragonflies
reminded me of wilderness canoe trips, with
the languid color and energy of littoral life.

This might be the perfect fishing hole, I thought,
though that would depend on our catch for the day.
Last time we baited our hooks, the one sunfish
Nathaniel managed to land didn't give us much
to celebrate…or dine on later. And today, so close
to a tangle of well-traveled roads, there was more
traffic hum in the air than I'd like, along with
the occasional rumble of a passing freight train.
But we could still hear the river. Feel the river.
Nathaniel had to use a borrowed pole, which dampened
his spirits a bit, but he enjoyed helping his friends
bait their hooks. The boys threw out their lines.

That was when we saw the first monarch,
imperial orange and black fluttering southward.
It had been two years since I had last seen one.
I had read they were close to endangered.
Then we watched another, and another, alight
for a nectar break on the far shore, then on ours.
Settling on leaves, wavering to and fro, up and down,
dancing along the stream. We counted twelve in all.
The fish weren't biting, but the boys were hooked
by the flittering monarchs. My heart leapt with joy.
The boys were excited by the harlequin quiver
of feather-light wings. The traffic noise faded,
the river current slowed and eddied. I can't recall
if we actually caught anything, or if we cared.

Driving home on a road flanked by the river
and the railroad, I imagined a parallel artery:
the aerial stream of the monarchs whose margins
had swept by us. I thought of other swaths of nature
in which we take unwitting part: shafts of sunlight,
ley lines, magnetic fields, the pull of gravity, the cycles
of water, weather and seasons. Factor in the pulsing
electrons that perfuse our lives and we find ourselves
engulfed by the fallout of our earthly transit.

The boys tugged me back to a more basic concern –
Auntie El's familiar farm and garden center, a reliable
way station with a bakery famed for luscious doughnuts.
Oh yes – the boys reminded me – apple turnovers, too.
It turned out to be a great day. Perhaps they all are.
We just need to take them in with different senses.
Lift our gaze, and listen for the shiver of wings.

Murmuration. What is that, anyway?
The faint babble of a woodland brook?
The gurgling seep of a compost heap?
The susurus of a stammering heart?

None of the above, I'm told,
but I saw my first the other day
as we drove along the thruway.
I *had* seen one before, though it
was only a pixeled simulation.
This was actual and feathered:
an undulating cloud of starlings,
swooping, twisting, tumbling,
spreading and shrinking, until
it rippled silently over the horizon.

A unanimous flock of thousands,
shifting with startling precision…
bending, folding and unfolding like
a winking mirage of northern lights,
thronged ever so tightly together
in split second maneuvers, yet
never, impossibly, never colliding.

Usually – I'm told, again – there's a predator
in the vicinity, and I did spy a soaring hawk.
Safety in numbers must be a *modus vivendi*
for starlings (or would that be *modus volandi*?).

Have I been looking the other way?
Is this only when they migrate?
How long do they stay like this?
All I know is, I've seen my first
murmuration, and it left me
murmuring in amazement.

EVANESCENCE

So much snow everywhere,
you doubt it will ever completely thaw.
Mounds, moraines, extravagant banks of it.
Side streets are narrow chutes of dingy white;
parking lots, hemmed with massive piles
of plowed and bucketed snowfalls…
on freezing, windy, overcast days
they are sierras of solemn, sooty,
obstinate ice. But nothing lasts forever
in this everchanging world. Or so I've heard.
The sooner we accept that truth, the happier
we'll be, free to live in the mercurial present.

Meanwhile, imperishable snows and crusts aside,
nature quietly makes her plans. By May, that
thick coat of dulling white in my backyard
will be gone entirely…the juncos at the bird
feeder will have flown north. The burning bush
will have all its leaves, and I won't be able to see
the house next door. The floor of the shaded
woods will be the last to surrender its gelid mantle,
and we will sigh to see winter's last glimmers
flicker and melt away…as the living earth
shrugs its adamant way into the blossoming air.

Nathaniel and I went to an upscale strip mall
on a last-minute quest for a Mother's Day gift.
In the parking lot we saw waves of fallen
white petals scooting along the blacktop,
whipped by the wind in all directions, some
blown into puddles where they caught and
quavered. We agreed they looked like snowflakes
that would never melt. And we wondered
where their final resting places might be.

Mission accomplished, we decided on dinner
at a family chain we'd never visited before.
We were shown to a table that had, like every
other table, a small black computer for checking
the menu, placing your order, asking for refills,
paying your bill and – before, during and after –
playing video games! Looking around the room,
I noted at every table where there was a child
– and ours was no exception – those games
were the main attraction. Parents were left
to stare into space, or maybe at one of the
dozen or more muted flatscreen televisions
that hung high on the walls around the room.
Some never looked up from their smart phones.
The setting was unappealing; the food, unexceptional.
I decided to try my hand at napkin origami.

The next day, Mother's Day, where our driveway meets
the door of our garage, a teeming mound of winged ants
appeared, hundreds of them, as hundreds more swarmed
off in every direction, back up the drive, under the door's
weatherstripping. Why or how they chose to be there,
I couldn't guess. None of them were flying. It was as if
their mother had just brought their wings that morning,
and they were being careful not to get them dirty.
I sat down on the ground and watched them.

For a moment's contemplation, windblown petals
and winged ants top digital dining rooms any day.

truth – how are you going to find it,
where and in what way define it

is it something here to stay
or just for now, an hour, a day

is there a base or bottom line
that will stand the test of time

business barons and politicians
disregard such propositions

if you want the truth for real
(and nothing but) this is the deal:

don't expect it from the courtroom
or a money-manic boardroom

hear, truthseeker, what I say
the truth is near, not far away

as nature sweetly manifolds,
abides, surrounds and gently holds,

clearly there, in streams that flow,
in flowers, seeds and all that grows,

morning mists, sunrise, sunset,
what you see is what you get –

birth and death, life and decay
it's all there, not hid away,

nature's beauty, joy and wonder
can't be disguised or split asunder.

to seek the truth, meet by the trees,
take counsel from the roots and leaves.

there you'll find how raw and free
the truth can be for you and me.

Once a conference speaker, an epidemiologist, had appeared
onstage standing before a blank screen. "I am now going to show
you," he had said, "the image of the person responsible for more
African deaths than any dictator." He pressed a button, and
on the screen appeared the face of Rachel Carson. Because
of her campaign to ban DDT, he said, the number of deaths
from malaria in Africa had increased tenfold.

    —MARY GORDON, *THE LIAR'S WIFE*

THE Rachel Carson? MY Rachel Carson?
She of *Silent Spring*, the slender volume that
spawned the modern environmental movement?
This gentle (or so I always assumed) person?
I've thought of her as a small, gray-haired woman,
peering through binoculars, inspiring children and
those who love them to treasure the natural world.
A poetic writer, much quoted – by me, among others
of greater repute – who made "a sense of wonder"
the watchword of thankful generations.

Rachel Carson, a mass murderer?
How your world can be shaken in the blink
of an eye. What is the truth here? Something,
somehow, has been overplayed or misconstrued.
My reaction, for one, as it turns out:
The Liar's Wife is a work of fiction, after all.
But it sounded plausible, nonetheless, that such
a judgment could have been imposed.

Apparently (thank you, Google), Ms. Carson
never proposed banning DDT in other countries,
nor even a total ban in our own. Certainly,
there was controversy, an outcry from
chemical companies. No surprise. But
she's back to being a hero in my eyes.
Shame on me for doubting.

Nature reminds us in so many ways
that she will not, can not be denied.
I think of the weeds that squeeze up
between the concrete barricades
that divide the hum of uptown and
downtown traffic on the Westside Highway.
At the red light, I see them pushing through,
and I silently cheer. As they, in turn, cheer me –
proving the earth is still alive and fecund
beneath the barren crusts of commerce.
She keeps breathing steadily in and out
under the avenues, all day and night,
unlike the spasmodic, irregular panting
of harried motorists crisscrossing her face.
I wonder how many drivers bother to notice
these resolute, respirant whispers of green.
We've come so far from the garden,
yet the garden continues to grow
up through the unfeeling avenues.

Thich Nhat Hanh held up a blank sheet
of paper and asked, if I remember correctly,
"Do you see the cloud? This is something
that exists right now. Before this manifested
as a piece of paper, it was already here
in the form of a tree, of the sun, of a cloud.
Without the sun, without the rain,
the tree would not have lived,
there would have been no piece of paper.
When I touch this piece of paper I touch the sun.
I also touch the clouds. There is a cloud
floating in this piece of paper.
You do not have to be a poet to see it."

Hearing this, surely I am not alone
in feeling as if he's speaking directly to me
No one – nothing – stands aloof, apart,
independent of anything, everything else.
Outside, looking up at an actual cloud,
drawing on all there is to inform my senses,
I still draw on what there is inside of me.
Looking first in a mirror, poet or not,
I spy the firmament of clouds within.

It will not be hard or sad
to bid goodbye to this winter
so prolonged and severe.
Still, as I make my way today,
remnant scabs of melting snow,
shrinking mounds and hillocks
plowed aside on roads and grounds,
haunt the landscape like strains
of a poignant winter requiem.
I watch them steadily subside
from silvery white to dismal dun,
from pristine knolls to drab moraines,
and can't but mourn their passing.
I wonder as warm days advance
what incidence of sun and shadow
will measure their disappearance,
as one plot diminishes apace,
another hangs on stubbornly,
and one by one they leave the ground
freshly scoured for spring to green.

Woke up to four or five inches of white,
skinned with an exquisite shudder of ice.
Every step we ventured began with
a crunch before we sank into the snow,
sending crystalline fragments skittering
in all directions over unbroken ground.
Our progress was strenuous, plodding,
percussive, and strangely lyrical.

The undulant, untrodden surfaces
begged to be left undisturbed. Still,
we couldn't resist flinging acorns or sticks,
like we were skipping stones across a pond.
As the morning air warmed, puffs of wind
knocked icicles from the unshadowed
branches of trees, and they clattered away,
frictionless, on the uneven, frozen terrain.

Watching the lively, colliding commotion,
the icefield a skirmish of smithereen ricochets,
you could see how curling became a sport.

We went out on an early May night,
boots on our feet, flashlights in hand,
in search of spring peepers
in the wetland by the barn –
frogs no larger than a thumbnail
whose mating-call pipings belie
their eensy amphibian size.

On warm nights these males
are so shrilly raucous
you can hear them over
a mile and a half away.
Here we were among them,
twenty-five stealthy stalkers
lit by a full-circle moon
reflected in pools of open water,
our flashlight beams stabbing the
shadows for peepers, our hands
cupped to catch one, if we could.
Now and then, an excited whisper:
Got him! All of us, otherwise,
even the youngest, oh, so quiet,
breathless in expectation.

Gradually, another serenade
accompanied our tiptoe pursuit…
a lower sound, a barely audible
purr at first, slowly, steadily
crescendoing until it was
a powerful, mesmeric drone…
until it seemed our bodies were
vibrating in sympathy, engulfed
by a solemn primordial chant.
"Is the earth humming?" a child
whispered. It seemed that way,
but these were the mating croaks
of toads — as if in throaty response
to the peepers' piercing calls.

Yet how much more novel, more
tinged with magic and mystery,
to conjure a humming earth?
The notes may sound utterly foreign,
yet somehow you know them by heart,
or you imagine that you do. Why not?
There is such sway in nature's canon.

If something catches your eye or heart,
stop right there, and spend some time.
Follow the fuzzy yellow caterpillar
that seems so intent on where it's going,
in such inchworm haste to get there.
Or watch that floating dragon-cloud
as it morphs into another chimera
before drifting apart or out of sight.

Stop. Close your eyes for two minutes,
then open them slowly…what do you see?
Has anything changed? What might you
have missed without that fresh awakening?
Listen to your breathing, feel yourself
draw the air gently in and let it softly out.
Then again…then again. And again…

We are visual beings much of the time.
When we see something, we keep
a virtual checklist in our heads – okay,
that's an oak tree, stout and handsome,
all right, got that, what's next?
But don't neglect your other senses
as you take your silent inventory.
Get close to that maple and smell
the bark, trace the margins of a leaf
with your finger, listen to the branches
rattling in the wind. Taste the sap in late
winter, then the syrup at sugaring time.

It's important to be comfortable
out of doors, so dress for the weather.
Don't forget to pee before you go,

so you can sit or lie motionless, gazing
with soft, relaxed, unfocused eyes
at what stands or moves before you,
and feel the world's immensity.
Then narrow your vision to focus
on the details. Back and forth, from
wide angle to macro, forth and back.

Share nature with your friends,
but don't get so lost in conversation
that you miss the natural moment.
Forget about expectations…your mind
should stay open to the unanticipated.
Go, and explore with "beginner's mind."
Go again, to see if you notice any changes,
or just because you feel the call. Go slowly,
whether or not you have a choice.
Then go more slowly still.

Visit a park with hiking trails
or lounge in your backyard chaise.
But do one or some other every day.
Put away your notebook and camera –
leave nothing between you and nature –
keep your diary in your heart.

As John Burroughs says, wait –
"The stars come nightly to the sky,
The tidal wave unto the sea;
Nor time, nor space, nor deep, nor high,
Can keep my own away from me."

A new family moved in across
the street, just two doors down.
We'd been waving to them in passing,
but had yet to extend any formal welcome
to the neighborhood, with or without
a housewarming gift or batch of brownies.
I had contemplated something like that,
but had done nothing about it, anticipating
some less structured opportunity would
arise for us to make our acquaintance…
sort of in the social ebb and flow, y'know?

Nature opened the door eventually.
I had tapped another neighbor's maple,
and sap was oozing neatly into the bucket
I hung there while I went home to fetch
an instruction sheet on how to boil what
was accumulating in the pail to make syrup.
Heading back, I hailed the new kids on the
block as they were playing in their snowy yard.
I asked if they wanted to see the tree I was tapping.
Go ask your mom, I urged them. She came
outside with two more kids in tow, and we
traipsed across the street together.

The kids were shy, but still fascinated by
the clear sweetness dripping out of that tree.
One tasted with his finger. The air was dulcet
with wonder, curiosity and smiles all around.
We returned to the street, where Mom
had decided to stay, wearing sensible shoes
unsuited for the snowy ground, and we
introduced ourselves as we recrossed the street.

That was all it took. The social ebb and flow,
as it happened, was the ebb of our wonted
reticence answered by the flow of maple sap.
We waved good-bye, exchanging thank-yous
and you're-welcomes. The ice was broken.
Next time I see any of them, I expect there
will be enthusiastic waves and halloos.
Nature brought us together for genuine
kinship and harmony. Gathered around
that bucket of sweetness, you might suppose,
we tapped the milk of human kindness.

It's March, the end of a long winter,
and snow still blankets our yard,
but the sap has begun flowing freely,
I spotted my first robin a week ago,
and we've been hearing of crocuses.
Stand out of the wind and you can
feel the reassuring sun soak into you,
warmth blooming your cheeks.

That's how it was when Nathaniel
and I returned home from school.
I glanced out the window overlooking
our courtyard entrance – where a sort
of micro-climate, enclosed on three sides,
marks the warmest niche of our property.

Nathaniel! I shouted: A new swarm of
insects just hatched in the courtyard!
He immediately ran outside to look.
They're already dancing! he cried.

Dancing! Enchanted and gleeful,
he remembered them from past springs,
knew their place in the circle of seasons:
Insects on the living air, roiling endlessly
up and down, from side to side, bobbing,
weaving, slanting…*dancing*.

That's my boy. May he never lose that
wonderment, and ever love the dance.

For an hour this morning
the snow came down gently,
as if strewn by a faraway hand.
The thinnest of lacy, feathery
flakes, stitched by an artistry
intent on perfect symmetry,
landing one by one atop
the carpet of white
already on the ground,
where they threw the sun's rays
back into the air, argent, brilliant,
then in coruscating rainbows.
Moving slowly amid these millions
of drifting, mirror-like diamonds,
flocked and bedecked by them,
was like being brightly among
the flashing, glistering lights
of a towering Christmas tree,
high and wide as the sky –
a solitary, sentient ornament
hanging on the branching earth.

Where or when are you out?

Anywhere, from backpacking in a national park
to sitting on your porch in a folding chair.
Someplace, anyplace in between, as long
as you take it all in, and take heed.

Any time, though a regular rhythm is good:
a moment's reflection while you're taking
out the garbage or retrieving the mail…
a stroll around the block… a half-hour's drive
after breakfast to your favorite slice of nature
…meeting a friend for lunch in the park,
or after dropping the kids off at school.
With your children on a sunny Saturday,
or whenever you think of it, whenever
nature calls (no no, not like that).

You could find it difficult to make plans,
but fit it into your life, rain or shine…
an hour here, five minutes there, if it's
all the time you have. It's no big deal.
Set your alarm, mark your calendar, take
a cue from your mood and breathe in
when you're flat out or just a bit down.
But the more you can manage to get out,
the more you'll find yourself wanting to go
again, looking forward to it, even needing it.
Nature is patient; she will wait for you.
But you're only shortchanging yourself
if you don't make the effort.

I've watched steam rise from blacktops
after a sudden summer shower...wisps
of cool evaporation lifting from hot asphalt.
But here, under the chill sun of early March,
in a parking lot just cleared of newfallen snow,
still pocked with wet and dry patches,
warmer mists were enveloping my ankles,
like curling tendrils of smoke about to
draw me away to a nether world.
They wound slowly, quietly, barely
perceptibly in one direction, as if
with a conscious, deliberate guile,
coaxing me to surrender and follow.
I might have worried where they'd take me,
but there was nothing sinister at play.
Just a whisper of morning magic,
a grace note to the lingering winter.

There was no frail shuddering
behind those solid wintry scenes
in spheres of shaken, drifting flakes
that swirled and came to rest serene.

I loved them when I was a child
and still do, right to this day.
I'll never be too old to shake them,
shake and watch them bank away.

But yesterday we sat within –
taken by complete surprise –
a globe that sifted all around us,
enrapturing our minds and eyes.

This was no optical illusion,
no off-my-meds hallucination.
At our son's late afternoon ball game,
in proud parental dedication,

I and my likewise patient wife
sat in beach chairs facing west,
where the sun was slowly setting...
only two more innings left.

A quiet settled on the crowd
as golden sunlight rayed and glowed,
the diamond field became all hazy
and, I swear, the ballpark snowed!

As if on cue, the cottonwoods
released a cloud of gossamer seeds
that fluttered weightless through the air,
borne on a gentle evening breeze.

The Santas, cottages and evergreens
of globes I shook when I was young
were now pitchers, umps and fielders
backlit by the gauzy sun.

The players stayed intent on playing,
though movements seemed to hush and slow;
the gloaming and the billowing seeds
echoed the spell I used to know.

For several minutes – maybe twenty? –
the world was flocked with fleecy white
as the day turned inside out
and set the milky stage for night.

There were no spaces where I usually park,
so I drove around to the back lot.
The stepping stones of slate leading
from there to my office were still rimed
with last night's snow and ice, brindled
by a morning of rock salt and shoveling.
Minding my step from slate to slate,
I stopped dumbstruck in mid-stride.
The dappling of frost and melt
had etched the next stone with a chalky
pattern of rootlet tracery, branching
in all directions, like brushwork vines
wrought by a skillful hand, all trailing
fixedly to encircle a solitary pebble,
the pistil of a startling winter flower.
Ten minutes later, I brought someone
to share the vision, but it was already
gone, leaving only stone on stone.
It had to be enough that I had seen
this fleeting mimicry of blooming.

I need to change my parking place
more often.

On Black Friday we went to the mall,
of all places. Don't ask. We had to park
far away, of course, which gave us a chance
to observe the parti-colored leaves – fallen
from the strangled trees dotting the lot –
that were strewn across the gray macadam
or cupped in concrete urns.

The trees were all but naked.
The crisp leaves that lay scattered
on the ground were curled down
at their tips, as if they were poised
for push-ups on fingers and toes.
When a gust of wind caught them,
they stood up at once, like soldiers
snapping to attention, and scooted
in serried ranks across the pavement.
When the wind died, they promptly
fell onto their curled tips again,
as if on silent command from an
unseen drill instructor: Drop!
And give me twenty!

When we left the mall two hours later
the leaves still trooped up and down,
but their ranks were joined by a ragtag
sentinel of gulls on the fringe of the emptying lot.
When a car drove toward them, the birds
sauntered insolently out of the way, then
calmly, unhurriedly reclaimed their posts,
all of them proudly facing the same direction.
A Black Friday brigade of leaves and feathers
in close order drill – regimental nature
saluting and carrying on…as they were.

Today I took some kindergarteners
on a frosty nature walk,
a hatted, hooded ramble through
a foot of snow as white as chalk.

Just seven days ago we'd had
seventy degrees of spring –
gentle winds and greening grass,
chirping robins on the wing.

We didn't let the days-old snow's
thick crust of ice deter or balk us.
Breaking through it was a blast,
made our going happily raucous.

Hanging icicles splashed colors
where the dappling sun shone through.
Sparkling diamonds on the ground
scattered sunlight rainbow hues.

Our crunching steps retraced a spiral
I'd stamped out the other night.
Above us, in the bright blue sky,
some turkey vultures soared in flight.

The children pointed me to this…
I clapped and laughed and showed them that.
We paused to listen, smell and smile
till it was time we headed back.

Then I thought I spotted something
beneath some bushes to my right.
We slowed as one, stole up to – what?
A shape in shadows…a trick of the light?

And there he was: one small, slight bird
peered at us, trembling. Fearful? No,
but a sad and lonely bird, hunched over,
wings drawn in tight. Anyone we know?

We saw a flash of orangey red
when he let his wings unfold a bit –
a robin! Yes, a definite robin,
though he didn't seem too sure of it.

Was he sorry winter wasn't over?
Was he here to herald a new season?
Was he dismayed that last week's spring
had left so quickly, without reason?

We encouraged him to soldier on –
friends will arrive as days warm up.
The snow will melt, the worms will crawl,
life will flutter, fly and hop.

We'll meet again, sad feathered friend.
Just wait, the next flock will appear.
Our eyes may strain to find you in it,
but you'll be there…spring will be here.

Season opener for the Rockland Boulders.
Nathaniel, three of his friends and I got there
an hour early for hot dogs, etcetera, claimed
our seats, and the boys took off for the playground
to kick around a soccer ball they brought along.
They had shrugged when I asked them
why they were bringing a soccer ball to
a baseball game. Why not?

The boys kicked and headed their way
through a rain delay, until the setting sun
finally poked through a break in the
mountainous clouds that darkened
the rest of the sky. As I hustled the boys
back to the bleachers, I mentioned the dramatic
skies were ideal for rainbows. Whereupon
we turned as one toward the east, and there
was a dim but definite half-rainbow! I looked
around to see if anyone else was looking
besides the five of us…not a one. As usual,
I wanted to shout, "Look, people! Look up!"
but I refrained, and it was gone in a minute.
I confess I was pleased, even a little proud,
to have my spontaneous forecast borne out
in real time. A home run. In my mind,
I pumped my fist and whispered "Yesss!"

The Boulders were tied 2-2 in the top
of the eighth when the sky tore open
once more, and the game was suspended
(not sure what that means) along with
the traditional opening night fireworks,
much to the crowd's dismay. We were
all soaking wet, laughing and shivering,
by the time we reached the car, but it
warmed up before too long. I drove through
sheets of driving rain from one end of the
county to the other, depositing Nathaniel's
friends at their homes along the way.

By the time we got home around eleven
we were nearly dry, and I slept better
than I had in weeks. It was a night
to remember. Nothing spectacular,
just everything special.

I suppose it was bound to happen, but I'm not happy about it,
not one bit. My son Nathaniel, 13 on his next birthday,
has begun pestering for a smart phone. Up 'til now,
he's had little to do with computers, tablets, video games
or wireless whatevers. We might watch sports on television,
but that's about it. He's been in a Waldorf School, where
minimal exposure to technology is a given, but no matter.
I'm angry at myself, schools, business, society, the whole
world for succumbing so readily to digital "reality," to the point
where our children regard cellular access not just as something
they want, but as a birthright, a *sine qua non* of their existence.

We are confounding our lives in ways we have yet to understand.
Call me a Luddite; go ahead, I can take it. My mind is closed
to the virtues of virtuality, as I rail at what I won't abide
but can't avoid, seeing kids riveted to screens and touch pads
that purport to unite them. but only insulate them from life.
I will not debate this, or cite research that validates my qualms.
Just look around at kids with cell phones, how their world changes.
If I could hitch a DeLorean back to before all of this started
and inoculate the world against this viral stain, I swear I would.
Have I gone off the deep end? Maybe so…but so what?
I feel strongly about this. In case you hadn't noticed.

So, will we give our son a smart phone for his birthday?
I'm tempted to say "over my dead body," but I won't.
Instead: Happy Birthday, Nathaniel! Your mom and I know
that entering your teens is a milestone. You're on the cusp
of manhood, and it will bring challenges that we trust
you'll meet with a level head and an open heart.
We're giving you the phone that you've been begging for,
though it is fraught with peril for you and your friends.
We worry that you'll want it with you always, that you'll
become lost without it. It's likely you'll bring it with you
to every meal, where it will sit by your place like a cyclopic
guest, and you'll check it constantly, lest you miss out

on some thing, somewhere, somehow. When a new version
is released, or the latest, greatest app, you won't want to be left
behind by the up-to-the-minute mob. Such things will matter
more than face-to-face conversations, more than the real world
of nature you have always loved so much. So many people,
young and old, seem to feel the actual world is failing them.
They seek consolation in pixels, or the Googling cluster
of netizens. Reality can't compete with the simulant tide
of augmentation. Want to know where that beautiful bird song
is coming from? Record it on your phone and an app will not
only tell you the name of the bird, it will link you to gigabytes
of ornithological lore, a universe of statistics. Who needs a flesh-
and-blood naturalist, or books, or maps…or the company of friends?
Friendship becomes a disembodied nexus; beyond that immediate
yet distant sphere the world is reduced to streams of information.
Your phone can record whatever is happening, so you can review
what you missed while you were busy taking pictures, and share it
with the friends you don't have time to visit. You can use up
every bit of the time you save exploring the screened world.

Truth be told, people don't own these phones. They're controlled
by them. You can't wait for your class or the school day to be over,
so you can check on whatever text messages, voice mails, tweets,
vines or instagrams you might have missed: the matrix of your most
umbilical relationship. Worried about losing it, having it stolen
or hacked, you may become anxious, distracted, disconnected
(amazingly), even depressed. There may be support groups,
but spiritual life will take a backseat to ghosts in the machine.

Your Mom and I love you dearly and want to be good parents.
We don't want you to miss out, to feel deprived or out of step.
So here is the phone you've been wanting so badly.
We sincerely hope you won't like it all that much.

We are getting wise to water…
too late, we're told, or none too soon.
There's a growing H_2O anxiety
that we can never get enough.
Droughts are becoming more common,
but on a personal level, it's reaching
the point where the faintest trace
of thirst is cause for alarm. God
forbid you should risk a parched
throat on your way. Wherever you go,
a bottle is your portable potable oasis.

On expeditions in years gone by,
hikers who were quick to complain
at the first hint of thirst could be
gently mocked for "water wailing,"
but we did bring along canteens –
flat, round tins in cloth pouches
that hung like heavy bandoliers
from our shoulders and banged
at our hips. We could hear the water
gurgling and sloshing, and it usually
tasted terrible. But we were glad
to have it. Water *is* important.

Today, though, we're all so accustomed
to having our needs met at once, even
the slightest thirst is intolerable.
So we have a plethora of options –
water vessels of all kinds, shapes,
sizes, colors and functions…
and names? (I'm not making these up):

Amphipod Hydraform Handheld
Nathan Speedraw Plus
Camel-Back 6L Groove with Built-in Filter
Nalgene Wide Mouth with All-terrain Cap BPA Free
Avex Pecos Autospout
HydraPak Stash 750 Collapsible
Light My Fire Pack-up
Hydro Flask Wide Mouth with Hydro FlipLid
Nalgene Everyday Glowing
S'Well – keeps hot drinks hot for 12 hours,
cold drinks cold for 24!
…and too many others to count.

Could all the options we have
in outdoor equipment, ironically,
be feeding our reluctance to go out…
suggesting it might be unwise or unsafe
to venture outside without "proper" gear?
Suggesting there's a *right* way to do it,
and you *must* have this gear and gadgetry
or risk your life? But there's no need
to make time spent in the open air
cluttered, complicated or whelming.
You don't need a protective bubble,
a hazmat suit or a dowsing rod.
You just need a little common sense
and a willing heart to whet your appetite.
And every now and then,
a sip to wet your whistle.

My first grandchild arrived today,
born to my eldest and his wife.
The embodiment of earthly love
on the threshold of vibrant life.

There is so much I don't know,
so much still to learn, and more.
If only she had words to tell us
where she has been heretofore.

Has she seen the face of God?
Did angels guide her on her way?
Did she choose her lucky parents?
When, where, how…and why this day?

Has she heard the heavens sing,
or lived other lives before,
touched the hem of cosmic being,
plumbed the bright sun's molten core?

How close to nature she must be,
eternities in her heart's beat,
spirit in matter no mystery,
secure in love free of conceit.

One thing I don't need to ask
as I gaze at her tender frame:
If anything is heaven sent,
it must be she. And thus she came.

LOVE IS A VISITOR
for Bill Daniel

usually
we don't think of her
we can't invite her
or force her
to come
to stay
fleeting moments
might be the best
we can hope for
she has her own surmise
brushes against us
for a moment
somewhere
out of nowhere
unaccountably
absent any notion
or summoning call,
yet in the rarefied air
about this goddess
(what else to call her?)
we somehow know
beyond reckoning
why our loved ones
are our loved ones
and will continue so
even though love
is a visitor

There is so much more awaiting us
when we step outside our doors.
It unfolds in glad profusion,
no walls or windows in the way.
Our senses spread with eagerness
to touch, taste, smell…and soar.
We may be drawn to far horizons,
but they never seclude us – they bring us
all together, closer. Young children,
with their cheering readiness to absorb,
quickly see how normal it is, how right,
to roam the ambit of the open air.

Even those inclined to regard nature
indifferent to any feelings or intuitions,
can't ignore all the data supporting the notion
that time spent outside is one of the best things
we can do for our vitality, for our children,
for our common good as well as the planet's.

Despite the wireless banding of social networks,
we find ourselves more disconnected than ever,
and sadly estranged from the world of nature.
"Natural" has become a commercial buzzword,
while nature herself and the times we devote to her
are increasingly fenced in, mined and managed.
Distracted and overscheduled by the shuttling
hurly-burly of survival, we live in air-conditioned
houses thickly set on treeless blocks, while nature
remains some other place, over there…if only we
had time to visit…maybe on our next vacation…
if we can afford it.

Don't believe it. There's much, much more.
Open your door, breathe in, and go out.

Mostly, I am unaware of standing on a planet,
a mote of Milky Way careening through the void.
Like most of us, I lack a solid frame of reference
for taking on such dizzying contemplations.
I read and sing about a blue marble circling the sun,
a spaceship earth resplendent in a garden universe,
but whatever I might think I grasp with my middling
mind, the reality remains, at best, a dim abstraction.

In the dark, cool round of Hayden Planetarium
I can lean back in a vibrating chair, gaze up at
a vaulted simulacrum of the heavens winking on and off,
while a sonorous, godlike voice resounds in my ears.
Planets veer toward and past me, orbit in and out of view,
meteors sizzle through the startled atmosphere, all is motion,
speeding, whirring, while the music swells and crashes
(as if all this spectacle needed tonal orchestration)!

Why not go outside at night, find a dark and quiet spot,
lie back and look up at the real thing? Believe me, I do.
I take in the silent splendor, the sweep of numberless stars,
but at such a distance the starry welkin scarcely moves.
I don't perceive the dynamic of wandering, spinning spheres.
I can get some feeling for it, nonetheless, when I ponder
the circling cycles and rhythms of earthly seasons,
the subtle, incremental maneuver of winter into spring,
the swifter, more decisive shift from night into day.
There are no godly voices, no symphonic scores or lights,
but there are whispers in my soul…and I'm thankful
for the complement of planetariums and planets.

My friend William always seems to have stories
to share. Most of the time they inspire me,
or set my mind to wandering, wondering.
The other day, as it was cherry blossom time,
he asked a friend who had lived in Japan
about the best place to see their luminous pink.
The answer was Kyoto. William calculated
airfare, hotel rates, time away from home…
and decided to ask someone else, who nominated
Washington, D.C. A long weekend would do;
he could drive there.

Then someone who grew up in New Jersey
recommended Branch Brook Park in Newark.
Getting closer, he thought, though he longed
to be reassured that wherever he chose to go
would have the *ne plus ultra* of cheery cherry blooms.
Then, in the midst of polling yet another friend,
he looked up at the tree under which they stood,
curious to know the source of the tiny pink
flowers that were falling on them. That's right,
it was a cherry tree. There just happened to be
a couple of lawn chairs nearby, so the two
of them spent the rest of that afternoon
in a conversation showered with blossoms.

Everything we need is present.
If we fail to notice, it's because we're not.
Present, that is.

On a cold, nasty, wintry-mix sort of day,
when a forever gray shrouds the lowering sky,
bear in mind that the sun is still shining,
bright as ever, right above the clouds,
just as it does in the luminous clear.
And if you're feeling as drab as the day,
picture that light beyond the clouds' ceiling,
throwing shadows along and across all below.
If you find yourself troubled within your own
shadow, remember that light – it is certainly there.
The stronger the shadow, the greater the light.

There's a song we sing at camp with a chorus
of "Listen, listen, listen to my heart song."
Sung in rounds, it weaves an ethereal mood.
If we listen, listen, listen for the earth's heart song,
we might not hear music so much as a muffled,
almost inaudible cry, strangled, faint, yet unmistakable.
We feel it more than hear it,
deeply, sadly, in our soul.

If our souls truly transcend our bodies
and interlace with others,'
then the cries of mother earth,
whom we injure so often,
must make it nearly impossible not to grieve.

Listen.

Can you hear her heart song?
How could we be deaf to it?
How can we atone for the harms
we have visited on our planet home?

Listen, listen, listen…

Is it now yet? the bumper sticker asks.
Well, yes, and yes, again yes…always.
We can't dwell on the past or future,
only mark the tick of time between.

Our lives are a pageant of moments,
of being 'twixt hope and regret,
filled with presents of presence,
ripe with the promise of our petty selves.

This means facing the world as it is,
muting the clamor of our thoughts,
forsaking preference or judgment,
becoming present, declaring "I am."

Saturday, as I worked the apple press,
making cider at the school's fall fair,
a sudden, silken breeze sprang up
and rippled through the nearby trees.

In an instant, glistening maple leaves
engulfed the grounds in brilliant yellow.
Everyone stopped and gazed in silence,
caught by the windswept pageant.

One and all, we let go of ourselves –
our plans and purposes, masks and stories –
took in the flurrying unfiltered (like our cider),
filled to the brim by the dappled air.

Later we found our voices and recalled.
We agreed it had been magical. Now,
how could it have been otherwise?

Nature is a theater of life and death and transition.
These are everywhere, no matter how slight:
the seedling that sprouts from a rotting branch;
the dessicated earthworms on the drive after a
rainstorm, swept there by life-giving rainfall;
the dead tree still serving as a home for birds,
raccoons, chipmunks, beetles. A caterpillar
with wasp eggs laid on its back, from which
the larvae, soon to hatch, will burrow down
and eat the caterpillar from the inside out;
the fallen leaves disintegrating to become
part of the nutrient forest floor; gossamer
webs shimmering with morning dew, mandalas
of wonder for us, mortal danger for other beings;
the enthralling palette of dying leaves as they
gently let go and take their time drifting down.
Do you know that if you stand still and watch
a leaf fall, no matter how far away it may be,
you will hear the sound of its touching down?

The two oak leaves – they were beautiful –
had served their purpose, suspended all summer,
photosynthesizing all day long. Until it was time.
Stretching outward from cramped bud quarters,
soaking in the light of the warm and enlivening sun,
looking at the world from on high; proud to be part
of a mighty oak. Then buffeted by winds, drenched
by rains, chomped on by insects, suffering rips and
tears, while insects laid an egg or two upon them…
until it was time.

Time, when changing temperatures and light formed
that frail abscission layer at the base of their petioles,
when gravity and the slightest breeze – or one gust,
or no air movement at all – did their thing. Now.
I wonder how they fell: twinned in a swirling vortex,
or singly, softly swaying to the ground beneath,
perhaps blown up, down, apart and away,
to touch the ground with whispered thumps?

Was there a grand plan that these two leaves
were to be a help to others, who had more time,
that everyone and everything might have its time?
Sauntering through the seasons (thank you, John Muir)
and paying attention certainly makes Ecclesiastes'
"a time for every purpose" ring true. Seasons come
and go, yet we rest assured that they will come again.
And each time spring comes around it will be different,
and we will be different…and the mouse…and Jane.
Maybe they will be gone elsewhere, maybe not,
maybe somewhere between maybe and not.

There's a phrase I use in the first week of camp
(it's not needed after that) especially at lunchtime,
to answer the question, "Where do I throw this away?"
I say, "There is no such thing as 'away.'" Everything
we claim to throw away ends up someplace on, in or
above the earth. Science tells us matter can neither
be created nor destroyed – but it can certainly change,
with time.

Growing up, when I looked up at the sky at twilight,
I remember seeing long, dark clouds – not threatening,
but fair weather clouds turning somber as the sun set –
and imagining they were people who had passed on.
I was both frightened and fascinated. I wondered:
Does some part of us become a cloud when we die?
Or do we, maybe, become winds, or the scents
of spring, or birds, or butterflies…or snowflakes?
I didn't know. I still don't, not really.
Though I believe there is a God, he hasn't let
me in on the secret of how he manages things.
The best I can do is to go out into nature in
search of hints and clues. Until it is time.

PARKINSON'S

I knew something was wrong.
Putting coins into a meter was suddenly awkward.

Rubbing shampoo into my scalp, my left palm sat feebly
on my head while my right hand did all the work.

Someone asked why I was holding one arm
"that way," as if it had been injured.

The same left arm wouldn't swing as I walked,
but hung limp and indifferent at my side.

Skiing cross-country, my left ski kept straying
stubbornly out and away from the track.

I could no longer smell or taste my food,
much less the perfumed air of spring.

Oddly, I was overly sensitive in other ways…
gradually, almost indiscernibly

uncertain, vulnerable, and only dimly aware
of…there!…a trembling in one finger.

Scared and weeping, I went to my doctor,
who sent me to see a neurologist

whose diagnosis, in five short minutes,
was so swift and unwanted I could barely hear it.

It took a while for the word to sink in. Parkinson's,
he said, close to apologetically. Parkinson's Disease.

The good news, he said with a warm smile, was that
it was progressing slowly. He called it "an indolent case."

Indolent. Like the shampooing hand on my head, the arm
that wouldn't swing along with my suddenly slackened stride.

Indolent. How can something that steals into your life
and robs you of your constant self be called indolent?

Get your affairs in order, advised the leaflet
I picked up in the doctor's waiting room
right after hearing my diagnosis.
I hadn't thought of affairs for years
(and those were of another sort entirely),
but what are my affairs now, I wondered.
Debts? A close-to-underwater mortgage?
My camp, steadily growing until it was staggered
by a recession that flirted with depression,
but on the upswing once again…knock wood?

That's about it: the house and the camp.
No IRAs, stocks, investments, golden parachutes.
I don't confess it casually, or with disdain,
but I've never dwelt much on money matters.
Nor have I lavished my earnings on vacations,
kitchen renovations, second homes or yachts.
They have gone to six kids, private schools, colleges,
medical insurance, mortgages, car payments, organic
food, charitable donations and taxes. And now
Jill's back in school, mapping out a new vocation.

Over the years, I've watched many friends ply their
industrious indoor careers while I took to the hills,
squiring children up and down, gathering sticks and pebbles,
building treehouses, following the hawks' migration –
a bit like the grasshopper vis-à-vis the ant in Aesop's fable.
The ant labored steadily to stock his winter cupboard
while the grasshopper lazed under the generous sky,
scratching out merry tunes on his fiddle. No surprise,
when winter came, who was the more comfortable.

Not that I've been plucking at a fretless existence.
I've worked hard, and managed winters well enough.
I've just had other priorities, other affairs that beckoned
my attentions. Those open-air matters, the accustomed
concerns of my vagabond mind and heart, now do
the same for me as the grasshopper's provisional larder.
A day in the out-of-doors puts all my affairs in order.

After you have exhausted what there is in business,
politics, conviviality, love, and so on — have found
that none of these finally satisfy, or permanently wear —
what remains? Nature remains.

— WALT WHITMAN

I know my disease is bound to progress,
but I'm still taken aback by the evidence
of changes encroaching, ready or not.
For a few hours, every other day or so,
I feel nauseous but not, feverish yet not,
before the dire signs mystifyingly fade.
I tire easily, need a nap most afternoons.
I get depressed, which depresses me more.
"Going down that old rabbit hole," my wife says.
I don't think bunnies go quite so far down.

I resist the notion of cutting back at work,
though I've had to, whether or not I choose.
I'm not too glum about that; I have to be realistic.
My body is beginning to sway on its own,
bobbing and weaving like Muhammad Ali…
there is no float or sting in either of us now.
I've become uncomfortable in crowded places,
and don't have much appetite for small talk.
Those who know me best have noticed
my forgetfulness, my unwonted lack of verve.
I sprained my ankle while hiking as I
was preparing for summer…which once
wouldn't have slowed me down much,
if at all…but it did…and it does.

And yet…

Warming days of spring have brought back
the relative ease of going out in shirtsleeves.
Maybe it's the contrast to my inner mood,
but I can't recall when there were more
flowers on the cherry trees. The slightest
breeze sends aloft billows of shimmering pink.
I can hear baby birds in their nests, and dandelions
seem to be erupting all over the place. Leaves are back
with a flourish, and with them the spreading shade.
The planting and weeding of gardens has begun.
It might seem early, but I swear I saw a lightning bug.
And worms, lots and lots of worms. The juncos
have already left for their summer latitudes;
spring peepers are once more chorusing at twilight.

All that's missing are the fertile scents of the season.
If only Parkinson's had left me a sense of smell,
my rescue from the rabbit hole would be complete.

Dopamine is a neurotransmitter,
or so I'm told. A chemical essential
to the firing of neurons in our brains.
From birth, our bodies fabricate and
release it with every pleasure or reward,
as a vital component of memory,
movement, behavior, cognition,
attention, mood, learning, sleep…
the list goes on. Having no better
explanation, I take the doctors' word for it.

Brimming with sexual pleasure or
sated with leisure or food, we scarcely
notice the dopamine trickling, seeping
into our animal minds, when we feel
ourselves right and at home. Without
this self-dispensed stimulant, though,
we are sluggish, estranged from our selves.

Our dopamine levels fall off as we age.
Again, there is no explanation. No one
is immune from this fact of senescence,
but some of us face it too quickly, too soon.
This is the plight of a Parkinson's patient,
seeking reprieve in meticulous diet,
exercise regimens, and drugs like L-dopa
that never quite make up the difference.
I measure my days by a rhythm of dosages,
supplementing what little remains of my
store of dopamine…energy…coordination.

The onset was gradual, as is my decline.
To this point, there is no more explaining.
But I take it on faith – though no doctor yet
has endorsed my considered opinion –
that a walk among gardens or meadows
or forests is a sort of rebirth that recoups
my dopamine dearth for the moment,
briefly restoring my somatic well-being,
resetting the barometer of my fettle.
I hold this to be true for everyone.
I know I'm right. Take my word for it.

*The best remedy for those who are afraid, lonely or unhappy
is to go outside, somewhere where they can be quite alone with
the heavens, nature and God....As long as this exists, and it
certainly always will, I know that then there will always be
comfort for every sorrow, whatever the circumstances may be.*

    –ANNE FRANK

Casey Kasem, the sage of Top 40, went missing.
His family had been squabbling over where
he should stay, with whom, who can visit, how long.
Barely a year after his Parkinson's diagnosis
he was already plagued by dementia.

Such stories appear in the news every day,
but lately they land with a wallop. Will this
be the track of my 'indolent' strain?
At support groups I look around the room
and wonder, trembling, where I stand in the lottery.

It turned out Casey had been staying
with a friend. Maybe he wanted respite
from the awkward chorus of sympathies.
Last week two local men with Parkinson's
dementia went missing. One was found
dead in the woods not far from home.
They're still looking for the other.
I look around and wonder.

I can't help but read internet notices
about valiant deaths following long battles
with Parkinson's. I never enlisted in a war;
I guess I was conscripted. As for bravey,
I have no idea how valorous I am, or can be.
Is there any more courage or virtue in a lengthy
siege than there is in a sudden quietus?
I look around and wonder.

I'll see what I can do today.
Maybe I'll be able to manage
five laps on cross-country skis
around the athletic field –
I'm told that would be a mile –
with Charlie, my canine companion,
his dark body a frolicking silhouette
on white, strands of icy spittle streaming
from his jowls, as he runs with such
boundless joy. How I envy him.

I used to ski trails in Harriman often,
up and down mountains, old mining roads,
through village ruins and iced-over swamps,
alone or with friends, in flashing daylight
or under the moon, mile after mile, with
hearty, galloping energy. Like Charlie.
Well, without the spittle. Mostly.

Now…a single, flat mile. No mountains,
barely a molehill. I still find that hypnotic
rhythm of kick and glide, kick and glide.
But a mile is about all I can muster.
A wonderful mile, all the same. A mile
that goes forward. That's where I'm going.
Forward. That's what I can do today.

The first time I went to a Parkinson's support group
I felt like a teenager in a bingo parlor. A motley
of aging men, many of them slouched uncomfortably
in wheelchairs, staring blankly ahead, mouths agape,
unspeaking, perhaps unhearing for all I knew.

A sunny, upbeat physical therapist had us do a few
basic exercises while we sat in our chairs – hands
over our heads, bending, stretching, limbering up.
I had been trying to keep up with trail runs, push-ups,
yoga – vestiges of my once normal and active life.
Looking around, I felt this group was not for me,
but I wondered if it was where I was headed.

That day I began a determined, if half-hearted, search
for some other place, without much luck 'til now.
Last night was my second session with a group
in northern Jersey. It would have been my third,
but I got lost last time in the maddening tangle
of roads crisscrossing Bergen County. They're bad
enough in daylight; at night, fugeddaboudit.

Thanks to the authoritative monotone of my GPS whatzit
(a leap of faith for me), I managed to get there this time.
A neurologist and movement specialist spoke to us
with matter-of-fact kindness, shared an abundance
of Parkinson's understanding, available therapies, and
her belief that current treatments, evolving day by day,
are making life with this dreadful, progressive illness
less daunting, not just survivable but livable, even enjoyable.
A far cry from my first slack-jawed exercise session.

I'll be calling her for an appointment in the morning.

STOPPING

"Sometimes you have to be stopped right there in your tracks
before you can see that all the beauty in life is right in front of you."
    —WENDY LUSTBADER

Stopped in your tracks – by disease or injury or death,
by loss of a loved one, a job, a home or relationship,
by any number of those curveballs life can throw your way –
that's an all too familiar and fitting figure of speech
for those whom Parkinson's has so rudely derailed.

It's a rare day when we aren't stopped in our tracks,
unexpectedly frozen in place by obstinate limbs,
unable to move in any direction, anchored to the spot.
It might take a minute or longer to regain locomotion,
and in that endless interval, beauty is too often forfeit.

I know when I freeze in this way my first thought isn't
"How rare and beautiful the world is in this moment."
Rather, "Shit. I hope I don't fall, that no one is watching.
When did I take my last pill? Move, damn ungainly feet!"

Parkinson's does slow you down…it also forces you
to forsake the fastness of routine, consigning time to
take in the goodness around you, if you can seize upon
the music, tenderness, friendship, harmony, nature –
the ineffable favor of experience, of just drawing breath.

I believe everything we need is right in front of us, or
so close we run the risk of overlooking it. So when *you* are
stopped in your tracks, by whatever means or misadventure,
consider what we tell the wandering, wondering children
at camp: "Open your mind and say, Ahh!"
I really need to take my own advice.

Remember those uneasy days
of Junior High and High
when a gross, unsightly zit
made you almost want to die?

My mother said it's nothing,
you can't stay home from school –
no one will even see it. What?!
Did she take me for a fool?

It was massive, swollen, shiny,
redder than the reddest rose,
picking the worst place to appear,
the tip of my pubescent nose!

I knew how kids at school could be:
one glance in my direction,
and they were sure to snicker
at my blatant imperfection.

Everyone would see it!
The word would spread like flames:
A reindeer came to class today,
and Rudolph is his name.

Yet when the day had ended
none of this had taken place.
How overwrought a teen could be
with a red dot on his face.

Now, with Parkinson's in play,
when my symptoms manifest,
I might be the last to know,
though many others may attest.

My posture could be cockeyed,
my head and shoulders asway,
my gait slowed down, unsteady,
Yet I feel perfectly okay.

What disconcerting news for me
– more of a sudden shock.
Oblivious to all these things,
how should I make them stop?

Will I even know my future self?
Only time, I guess, will tell.
For now, living in the moment
is what's required, and just as well.

Not mortified, as with that pimple.
Just as I am, that plain and simple.

Recently some friends suggested
that there's someone I should see:
a special man, a chiropractor,
four short miles away from me.

I've been to chiropractors some,
to get adjusted on my way.
But now I'm faced with Parkinson's,
what could a chiro do or say?

Just go, they urged me, go and see;
it's not easy to explain.
There isn't much you stand to lose,
and might be so much to gain.

So off I went, and found the office
unpretentious, tucked away,
nothing fancy or portentous,
I'd drive right by another day.

Inside, I filled out two short forms –
that's it, surprisingly, no more –
found a chair, opened my book
and waited by the ominous door.

In three short minutes, he came out,
said he recognized my name
(he'd come to maple sugaring –
my sweet, familiar claim to fame).

Beyond the waiting room, he asked
about my Parkinson's disease.
The chronically ill do come, he said,
in search of etiologies.

Stretched out on his examining table,
I felt his firm but gentle touch

moving up and down my spine,
prodding my viscera and such.

He was silent, patient, thorough,
sat me up and smiled at me.
I know what's wrong, he said at once:
It's clearly, plainly mercury.

Mercury toxicity:
On dentist visits all these years,
your silver amalgam fillings have
been fifty percent Hg, I fear.

Not good, he said, and sent me home
with three prescription vials in hand.
"One supplement each day from each;
in two months, we'll see where we stand."

And most importantly, he warned,
make sure you drink a lot of water
to help this toxic mercury
leave your liver as it oughtta.

I Googled mercury, of course,
soon as I could, and sure as hell,
Parkinson's and mercury ingestion
share symptoms…antidotes, as well.

Will I get better? Time will tell,
as my hepatic mercury leaves.
Miraclous cure or medical hoax?
I don't know what I should believe.

But to quote the earnest friends
who counseled me on chiropraction,
What do I have to lose? Besides,
what's to be gained by bland inaction?

The Atrium is an elegant space, an unexpectedly
cozy chamber of high ceilings and skylights, furnished
with comfortable, sectional chairs and couches, wood
accents, plants and flowers (some, admittedly, merely silk
semblances tucked away from natural light, but still lovely),
marble floors overlaid with handsome rugs. A bright room
with a large fountain at one end that burbles with the sound
of cascading water, its walls adorned with paintings and
punctuated by tall windows that look onto the riverine
landscape of the Hudson Valley below.

A central partition displays what at first appear to be
photographic still lifes of untrammeled nature –
meadows flocked with wild flowers, autumnal hills,
snowcapped peaks – until the scenes slowly,
subtly transmute, the plants sway in unfelt breezes,
streams ripple, and perspectives slip and slide
almost imperceptibly, merging and emerging,
fading seamlessly one into the next...while pacific,
mellow music murmurs softly in the background.

Modest, unobtrusive banners hang from the rafters,
emblazoned with uplifting words and phrases:
Spirit...Rally...Renew...Heal...There is always Hope....
Similar messages appear along the roads and parking lots
of this Helen Hayes Hospital complex where I go
for wholesome sanctuary and all sorts of therapy.
How fortunate to be living only half an hour away...
I have time to arrive early for my appointments,
to drive past those inspirational signposts, to bask
in the solace and contemplative aura of that Atrium,
to gaze at the lap dissolve partition or out the window.

Today I sat next to a woman who was taking
it all in as I was; if we spoke at all, it was always
in hushed tones, until it was time for my appointment.
Many others passed through, not a few with walkers
or in wheelchairs, some missing limbs, some leaning
on a companion, their steps faltering soundlessly
on the carpeted marble. They have been brought
here by strokes, accidents, tumors, joint replacements,
perhaps a birth defect, or a progressive disease like mine.
All of us, brethren in the collective of infirmity.

Along one wall there's a photo essay devoted to the
hospital's history and the actress whose 1960's activism
convinced the state legislature to keep the hospital here,
not move it to Albany. She made her case in a letter
to the governor: "The sight of a tree, the view of the
Hudson, is as much therapy for our patients as the fine
treatment they receive…patients need to know that life
is worth living, that there is something outside
that they must struggle to get back to."

To which I can only add, "Amen. And thank you."

Parkinson's comes with all sorts of affliction:
pneumonia, hallucinations, aches and pains…
and now the urinary tract infection (UTI)
that my doctor tells me I may have developed.
Next week's test results will likely confirm it.

When I shared the news with a friend,
he smiled reassuringly: "I've got the solution
right here in my pocket." With a flourish
he proffered a packet of powder –
1200 milligrams of pulverized Vitamin C
to be stirred into water and gulped down at once.
Keeping faith with my friend, and Linus Pauling,
I swallowed. It's too soon to tell if it's working,
or how many more doses might be required,
but I already feel that my tract must be better…
which sets me wondering, as I so often do:

How many modern maladies could use
A packet of soluble recouping powder?
For being stuck in traffic, for lack of time
spent in the company of friends,
for dreading a visit to the dentist, for
a dismal day you think will never end.
Packets for stress, regrets, worries,
wearying weather, tedium, doubt,
the endless checklist of choking strife,
and above all, anything barring the way
from care for the soul. We all need
our portion of soul food, if you will.

Our soul may succor mind and body,
but it needs taking care of as much as
– no, more than – our insistent frames.

There is no prescription, no tincture, no pill.
Only…

Smile at everyone you meet…
tread the morning dew in bare feet…

pluck some flowers just for you…
lie down – look up at skies of blue…

or a sky awash with stars at night…
don't curse the darkness – be the light…

for a feast of soul-fulfilling food,
walk softly 'mid a forest's mood…

sit by a stream, watch dragonflies play…
don't just skim a book, read it all in a day…

hug a tree, looking up, and lean there a while…
crush a fistful of autumn leaves, smell them and smile…

watch fallen leaves whirl across the ground…
build a shrine from treasures of nature you've found…

plant a garden in your yard, or herbs in your room…
let the afternoon sun put an end to your gloom…

call someone, as you've been meaning to do…
dance, when the first snowflakes settle on you…

There's so much nourishment out there,
to keep your soul well-soothed, well-fed.
When your world feels heavy or bereft,
think of all there is to "eat" instead.

In *Mrs. Robinson*, Paul Simon asked,
Where have you gone, Joe D.?
Lately, I'm compelled to add,
and what of you, Ed B.?

I've always been six feet, two inches…
a reliable, statistical measure…
a solid, sturdy, manly stature
I vainly imagined I'd keep forever.

But at my last physical the nurse,
reading my chart, then eyeing the tape,
announced I was five feet, eleven and a half.
I said there must be some mistake.

How could I not even reach six feet?
I was saddened, shocked, dismayed.
Where did over three percent of me go?
Impossible, can't be, won't accept it, no way.

Double checking her measurement,
she sighed, "I'm afraid it's true,
but we all shrink a bit with age,
and so, at seventy, have you."

A "bit" I can reckon with, but two
and a half inches?! How can that be?
I can only attribute my new partner Parkie.
How he relentlessly subtracts from me.

Thus am I shorn of my vertical pride,
and my once high esteem is left wanting.
I now have more reason than ever to find
that the wages of life can be stunting.

If I'm with nine-year-old Nathaniel when my meds
start to taper off or I didn't take the next dose on time
and my gait begins to stutter, freeze or lurch,
he will whisper, "Sit down, Daddy."
The second time, "Sit *down*, Daddy!"
If there's a third time, he doesn't hold back:
"Daddy! *Sit Down!*"
He sounds angry. Most fathers don't do that.
Even though we've explained my condition,
seeing it suddenly hobble me has to be scary for him.
If his friends are over I imagine it must be embarrassing.

The most I can do is continue to be the best Dad I can,
as I've always tried to be. It's easy enough to get downcast,
to feel sorry for him, for me, for all of us. But for his sake,
if for no other reason, I refuse to go there. Nathaniel
is doing very well, thank you. He loves school, has friends,
smiles a lot, builds forts in the woods behind our house
(how lucky we are to have them). In the spring
he checks on the praying mantis egg sacs to see
if any have hatched yet. In the summer he comes
joyously to my camp. He knows when the juncos
have returned in the fall, and considers the world
a wonderful place. Above all, he knows he is loved
by his brothers and sisters and, of course,
by his Mom…and by his Daddy.

"Making progress" or "Coming along"
are noncommittal, not very real.
For now, a smiling shrug could serve
for general appeal.

"What's happenin'?" I might respond –
that just dodges the question, no good.
Too breezy, as if I'm movin' on up
like the Jeffersons in the 'hood.

With new symptoms come new queries,
the looks of me make clear the tale –
more stooped and herky-jerky, nodding,
sometimes falling, faint and frail.

Indoors I have my steady aches:
Neck. Shoulder. Elbow. Fingers. Knees.
Always favoring my left, I note –
my politics and pangs agree.

Years ago, when I was asked
if there were pains with my disease,
I could say no, not yet, perhaps
not ever – never, if you please.

Parkinson's can differ widely,
folk to folk or case to case:
muscles spasm, twist, contort…hurts
come and go and leave their trace.

More tired, weaker, slower, I struggle
to turn in bed or rise from the floor.
Depression, anxiety linger longer;
vulnerability runs up the score.

Looking back, all of these complaints
make for one long, daunting statement,
but I keep in mind, try to remember:
for every plaint there is *some* treatment.

By the way, if you're wondering about
my figments, delusions and sleepless nights,
they come and go; I make adjustments;
as I take my inventory of blights.

When Linda Ronstadt, a siren favorite
of younger days rootless and carefree,
announced her Parkinson's diagnosis,
she also said she would no longer perform,
making the unexpected assertion that
"anyone with Parkinson's can't sing."

I wasn't aware of this.
For years I've been belting out
songs every summer at Camp –
*This Land is Your Land, Father Abraham,
The Grand Old Duke of York*, strains of
time-honored campfire chestnuts.
After I'd been diagnosed, I saw and heard
no reason to hold back on my usual
full-throated gusto for joining the chorus,
and no one has complained – though
they may be too polite…or tone-deaf.

Granted, my warbling has never compared
to Linda Ronstadt's in her dulcet prime,
but I'm reminded of the bumper sticker
plastered on the back of my car:
Don't Believe Everything You Think.
That goes as well, I'll warrant,
for what you think you can or can't do.

There is more that I *can* do, still,
than there is that I can not.
It may not be easy to keep on,
but the choice must be mine.
I can be Eeyore — Woe is me! —
or Winnie — Let's go explores! —
or anywhere between. Or
all the above in a single day…
or in one mercurial moment.

Don't Worry, Be Happy
is another fireside favorite.
Amen to that. Now, more than ever,
happiness is a welcome companion.
I say, lift your voice to say, "Yes!"
And, by God, I'll sing if I want to.

I finally took out my cross-country skis for the first
time in four years, prodded by my wife and all this
snow on the ground…and Charlie in tow. We made
a few rounds of Mary Dailey Field (Charlie just bounds
all over, never mind the track). In no time at all, I found
my balance, got into that old rhythm of kick and glide,
kick and glide, and worked up a sweat. It felt great.
No one ever told me cross country was contraindicated
for Parkinson's, so after this run I have to recommend it,
for myself anyway. I can't wait to do it again tomorrow.

As Jill was sitting on the bleachers, she noticed the snow
pillowed on the bench below her not only looked
like a sponge, it actually felt like one. She pointed it out
when I came around again, and I could have sworn,
feeling with my eyes shut, that it really *was* a sponge.
Never experienced that before. My mind quickly sought
for an explanation: Let's see…the metal seats absorb
the sun's heat more from above, less from below,
then cool overnight. The snow's been here about
two days—Stop! Thinking! Just let it be, ignore
that insistent, inner, inexpert would-be scientist.
Keep it simple: "That's…really…cool."

Later, I attended my first session of a movement class,
Delay the Disease. It went well…the instructor
knew what we needed, and I'll be going back. Clearly,
exercise does slow Parkinson's down. Though I've reveled
in physical exertion all my life, I haven't done so much
since Parkinson's came to stay, excusing myself as too
tired, too busy, just getting through a normal day
is taxing enough. I can get exhausted cleaning house,
gardening, shoveling the driveway. I manage to fit in
a few hikes in Harriman, but not with the regularity
and sense of purpose that used to drive me. I need to
get back on the aerobic track again, on my skis,
with Delay the Disease, or whatever. I really should.
Yesterday, today and tomorrow, Parksinson's won't
be taking any days off. Keep it simple, keep it up.

Most of us live in Rockland County,
so it didn't take long to decide on a name.
Not that our men's group needed a name.
We just thought we ought to have one.

We've tried other epithets over the years
from 1976 to the present – yikes! –
that's quite a run, and it continues.
We settled on a rugged moniker,

intimating strong, stable, durable
individuals, maybe even a little "tough,"
though that would never be our bearing,
not even when we started

our monthly outdoor coven, talking
as we rambled craggy woodlands,
under the full moon if we could
(a brotherhood of lunatics).

We began around the same time
that women's groups were suddenly
everywhere, raising consciousness,
raising hell. Good for them, we thought.

Good for us. We had to be
curious men, questioning men,
or so we imagined, asking what
is a man, what does a man? Why?

Some of us were there for support,
wounded by lost love, divorce, solitude,
in search of a certain something that
we couldn't quite put a finger on.

Hard to say, today, if we're any closer
to knowing where to put that finger,
but the years have been worth our while,
our vying to reckon with the riddle.

As you might expect, the years
have taken their toll in sundry ways.
Our number has fluctuated somewhat,
but we've been fairly steady. Rockmen,

solid, like the subjects we pursue
each time we meet, at the discretion of
our chosen leader for the night, whose muse
can be as random as he likes. We follow suit.

Our hair, what's left of it, is mostly
gray now, along with our beards.
Men seem to favor whiskers all the more
as their thatches thin on top.

We've all contended with chronic ailments,
like the Parkinson's that has been my
obtrusive companion for the last fifteen years.
I am changing, rockily. But who isn't?

Last night, the pills that keep Parkie at bay
seemed to have little effect, as I staggered
and stumbled, determined to keep up. I had
no intention of quitting – or breaking my neck.

My fellow Rockmen weren't about to let me,
surrounding me with urgent arms and hands,
reaching out with all the wary vigor
they could muster. A true support group.

But most bracing of all were their hearts,
their encouraging words, their careful,
watchful eyes cradling and coaxing me,
enclosing me in a circle of safety and grace.

Last night, at least, I was certain about
what we've been trying to put our finger on.
From so many shoulders, hearts and hands,
I felt the patient love of fellowship.

Rock solid.

I was depressed when I woke up this morning.
Down, though a sunlit new day was just dawning.

Anxiety furrowed my woebegone face –
I needed another, a different space.

At the cafe, I thought, on its deck at the front,
alone with my coffee, what more could I want?

So I went. (I tell everyone nature is healing...
out-of-doors is a balm for whatever you're feeling.)

Come on, Nature! I challenged the fresh morning air...
perk me up, but I'm not going to move from this chair.

The sun, as it climbed in the clear eastern sky,
became like a spotlight that drew my glum eye

To some cones clustered high on a Norway Spruce tree –
it set them all glowing (it seemed) just for me,

Kissed with a gold that I'd not seen before.
There's one spark, I allowed, but I need some more

(My mom used to say that good things come in threes....
That means two more to go, that's what I want to see.)

A sudden wind nudged a large leaf 'cross the deck
until, when its petiole caught in a crack,

it stood up straight like a proud semaphore
and stuck there. I marveled. OK, that's one more.

Then I thought about who I might like to stop by –
my mind settled on Ray, a companionate guy.

Minutes later, someone happened along on a bike.
Sure enough, it was Ray, slowing up to say "Hi."

So we talked. I felt better. It was a new day:
The sun's rays, a leaf raised and a visit from Ray,

proof again of the worth of my wonted advice:
Time spent out-of-doors will ever suffice.

We went on a winter retreat in the Catskills.
Two days and nights of snow and more snow,
huddled around a great wood stove, cocooned
in warmth as the flakes fell and fell outside.
Away from our usual lives for perspective
on last summer's camp in review, on what's
working, what isn't, what needs tweaking,
and what could be new for next year.

We talked through details, drew up a timeline,
worked as the team we have been for so long,
carefully on the same page, with mutual respect,
friends as well as colleagues, committed to making
a difference in childhood summers…and our own.
We decided this year our watchword should be
what we owe to the earth and each other: Gratitude.
Our communion was close and exhilarating.

Back home, exhausted, a bit off my meds, I proceeded
to fall in the hall, snapping my walking stick in three.
Without it, I might have done the same to my arm.
Instead, I injured my pride far more than my body,
dismayed to mark my return with such a lame spectacle,
putting my family on tenterhooks. I worried that
Jill might be upset with my long days of working for
camp having left me bereft of reserves…and Nathaniel
must wish Daddy wouldn't tumble like that.

We ate dinner in virtual silence, then straight to bed.
Nathaniel crept in to lie next to me: "Are you okay, Daddy?"

When we awoke the next day Jill was aloof at first, before
speaking her mind in the typically forthright manner I have
come to admire, even rely on. She was close to overwhelmed,
she said, by bickering children, cooking and cleaning, cold
and snow and…well, *everything*. I just knew that final,
emphatic summation included me — and the burden
of Parkinson's she was forced to share.

Nonetheless, I had to prepare for our first maple sugaring,
assembling buckets, spouts, hammers, projector, hand-outs.
Conditions were perfect: warm days after cold overnights
meant the sap would be flowing when we tapped the trees.
The prospect of syrupy success made our task easier,
distracting me, for the moment, from tensions at home.
Nathaniel and Daniel were with me – my two maple boys.

On the day of our workshop, the sap oozed on cue,
children and parents gathered 'round, eager and smiling.
Nature poured forth the promise of another bright spring.
Falling down and falling out with Jill were still on my mind,
but the delectable sap was like oil on troubled waters,
reason enough for gratitude…and hope. Always hope.

The day after hiking the RD Trail on Blackrock Mountain,
I was so besotted by what I'd seen, I wanted to share it with Jill.
Life has been hectic lately, with so little time to connect.
Why don't we go there tomorrow, I said. She gladly consented.
In the morning she wasn't so keen, but we stuck with the plan
and brought Charlie along for some comic relief.
She was tense, terse, not herself. We barely spoke in the car.
As Eddie the Ever-Alert-to-Relationship-Cues Watchdog,
I sensed all was not well in the state of our union, matters were
somehow amiss with my life's boon companion. We parked
at the trailhead and began to hike, my stomach in knots.
Charlie bounded ahead, oblivious to our disaffection.

Scarcely five minutes along the trail, as we were entering
a woodland valley, Jill broke into tears. I'm angry, she shouted,
and sad…and frustrated. For days she'd felt as if we were
barely roommates, sharing a house without really sharing
our lives and, really, no love. Parkinson's, she said, has been
like a thief, stealing scraps of her even as it tore at me,
a little at a time…stealthily, heedlessly, implacably.

It was beauty that breached the wall of her discontent –
taking in the splendor of where we stood, remembering how
we used to come to Harriman and hike much more often,
just the two of us, with or without Charlie, maybe with the kids.
We hadn't been doing that lately, and she was sad about it.
As we talked, I got so upset I felt like turning back.

But Jill said we should follow Charlie, already yards ahead as usual.
I agreed with heavy steps, but I gradually lengthened my stride,
the mood between us began to lighten. The time and place
had captured us, goaded us almost physically, whispered to us:
keep climbing. Now and then we stopped in silent unison
as the leaves fell and fluttered around us. Nature's precincts,
once again, compassed a healing, enthralling release.

The top of the mountain was shrouded in mist. We sat down
to watch it, to feel it pass through us in translucent waves.
If we waited for the sun to come out, the mist would vanish
and we would be able to see a far, forested 360 degrees from
our perch. We couldn't wait, though, and headed down feeling
quite differently than we had at the start. Despite the curtain
of fog, we knew the world was still there, and the sun would
shine brightly once more, without a shadow of the thief.

Deep Brain Stimulation, the doctors had said
could be just what I needed. I said, go ahead.

They started by drilling two holes in my dome
for wiring electrical impulses from

a battery pack planted high in my chest
intended to jump start my rhythm and zest.

A week later they turned on the juice just a jot
Any difference? they asked. I answered: Not.

In three weeks I went back for a slight upward tweak
Notice anything yet? I shrugged: not for weeks.

Be patient, the doc said, it can take months before
you feel any changes. I was hoping for more

and sooner. But people I'm running into
tell me they notice new life: "A new you!"

So it may be working, just so slowly and subtle
it would be premature in this moment to scuttle

the whole undertaking. After all, it took years
to develop this business; I'll let go of my fears

and let science decide if this shot at the moon
will land where I hope it will. Patience. Stay tuned.

It seems I was jumping the gun a while back
when I said there were signs of improvement.
For a day here or there, maybe, but I would fall again –
you should see my knees! – and wonder despondently
if this was going to be my life. Things seemed to be
headed downhill for the last month. I kept telling
my doctor I was a mess at home…falling more, miserable.
I went to my Tuesday appointment insisting that something,
anything, had to be done. She eyed her control unit warily…
and discovered — I wasn't even plugged in! No current
was making its way to the electrodes in my brain —
for anywhere from the past month to the entire time!
I asked if this had ever happened before. Once, she said,
but it was clear right away the woman wasn't plugged in
because her shaking had come back so quickly.
My issues were less obvious, more episodic: posture,
balance, swaying. I was glad there was a reason for
the way I felt, but I had to wonder how they had checked
to be sure the system was on in the first place. Shouldn't
someone have picked up on my uncoupled status?

Once I was finally, properly turned on, one night was enough
to mark the difference – steady, stable, no shaking, no depression.
I got lots of work done on Wednesday without tiring – not my
old self yet, but inspired, slightly hyper, ready to tackle the world.
This morning, at Helen Hayes Hospital for physical therapy,
my therapist couldn't believe I was the same person. I know
I have a long way to go and need to take care of myself. I still
get a bit shaky at night. But, hey—I've only been "hot" for three days.

Here's to cane-less, walker-less Eddie, a little behind
schedule, perhaps, but glad to be a part of the world again.

The past four days I have been walking, early or late,
without any tendency to trip or freeze in place,
no need for help getting through doorways.
I have been, dare I say it, fully, fitly, blessedly ON.
NO staggering or festination (hurried little steps).
Unafraid of falling, I look normal as I make my way.

On my last office visit, the doctor adjusted the electrical
flow from the batteries in my chest and replaced two
of my meds with new ones. Could these changes
be making the difference? I'll keep my new walker,
of course, but it may be years before I need it again.
I feel like the whole world is re-opening to me.
I have more energy than I've had in a long time.

Yesterday, where I plan to sow wildflower seeds in my garden,
I laid down sheets of black plastic to inhibit the weeds
that have been coming up, so the wildflowers won't face
any competition. When I ran out of plastic, I went straight
back to Home Depot for more, no problem. A week ago,
even one such trip would have been a real stretch – getting through
the automatic doors without halting in my tracks, pushing the cart
without juddering, sadly aware of unwanted attentions.

Today I have an Open House at camp. I won't have to struggle
to hide my tremors by sitting down before the parents and kids
enter the room where I'll be showing slides — I can meet them
confidently at the door. I don't know if this is a fluke or how long
it may last, but it's wonderful to feel sure of myself again —
clear-headed, in balance, coordinated....Ohhh, this feels good.

For the past month people have been telling me
how good I look. Seriously. Without any
prompting or subtle glances for reassurance.
Our HVAC mechanic who still remembers,
like it was yesterday, when he learned
all about maple sugaring in third grade.
A camp mom, after the summer slide show.
A clerical worker in the Main House,
where we have our year-round camp office.
So many volunteer, unsolicited affirmations,
I'm beginning to think they might be right.
I'm not about to argue with the facts.

I guess it's safe to say my DBS procedure
was successful. My dyskinesia – involuntary
movements, tics, bobbing – is all but gone.
I'm sleeping well, I move around pretty easily,
I don't feel like I'm about to fall all the time
…except, maybe, after 8:00 pm. But I'm able
to hike again in Harriman State Park! That,
alone, is enough to put a smile on my face.

All in all, then, my Parkinson's symptoms
seem to be under control, though I've noticed
my handwriting has been getting worse —
when I try to take notes, they're impossible
for anyone, even their author, to decipher.

I make many more typing erorrs, and speaking
up is an occasional unwonted trial: stumbling
over the simplest words, I wind up spewing
a rapid-fire stutter, like Porky Pig at The End
of a Looney Tunes cartoon: Th-Th-The,
Th-Th-The, Th-Th—That's all, Folks!

There continue to be times when I'm a bit "off,"
when my gait goes abruptly herky-jerky, or I
keel over, or swing and sway, or can't stand still.
I'll get the shakes all of a sudden, or freeze up
as I'm about to take an unimpeded stride.
Every now and then I'll hallucinate (wait,
is that tree actually dancing the hula, or what?).
I can get unaccountably tired, and my posture…
well, let's just say runway modeling is out,
not that it was ever in. Balky bowels demand
daily prune juice, apples and plenty of water.
And patience.

When I start listing all these things, it might sound
like my glass is more half-empty than half-full.
But, hey, people say I'm looking good…and I
feel good enough to believe what they tell me.

A LETTER

*Every year I receive some Christmas cards that include a
year-in-review — often a typewritten letter on a separate sheet
of paper, single-spaced, front and back — with thorough details
of family life, the comings and goings of extended relations,
friends and neighbors. They cover birthdays, weddings, anniversaries,
funerals and other rites of passage, as well as travel itineraries,
medical crises, dietary changes, culinary experiments (like that
disastrous, pancaked soufflé)…and updates on the arrival and
departure of family pets. Much of this, frankly, might fit the
category of Too Much Information, but I read every word —
and confess to relishing these bulletins from beyond my doorstep.*

*Herewith, a New Year's Day letter. If you find it tedious
and boring, just skip it. You've finished the book anyway.*

Dear Everyone,

*I hit a bump in the road this past fall. More like a collison with
a Mack truck, to be honest…though I do not remember any of it!
I came down with a classic case of — get ready for this mouthful —
Acute Metabolic Encephalopathy. Try saying that quickly, three
times in a row. I'm told I became psychotic, and had to be
restrained in a hospital bed, if you can imagine that.*

*How did I come by this tongue-twister? A nasty interaction
between some of the drugs I was taking (all legal, of course), bad
enough to have me hallucinating and thrashing about for two days,
until it was safe to move me to a rehabilitation unit at Helen Hayes
Hospital for three weeks of speech, physical and occupational therapies.
There I gradually recouped my ability to walk, think and remember;
the hallucinations were slowest to subside. My meds, meanwhile,
were cut from fourteen to five pills per day. How the pill count
got so high, I'll never know.*

*I've decided not to drive anymore. Too iffy. I had already had
a few close calls, even before this latest awkward episode. They sent
me home with a walker. (How's that for a trade-in: A car for a
walker...I have always driven a hard bargain.) The inconvenience
of losing my familiar automobility has been greatly eased by many
kind souls who are quick to offer a ride when I need one. My
outpatient therapist at Helen Hayes says I should be able to
lose the walker by the end of her ten weeks with me — yay!
Other therapists working with me are confident of bringing me
back to — or ahead of — where I was before I went off the rails.*

*As far as my Parkinson's prognosis is concerned, there continue to be
some good days and some bad, depending on my frame of mind, mostly,
whether or not I'm getting enough sleep, my level of anxiety, financial
concerns or what have you. I can get depressed or frustrated; my gait
is generally "funny;" and the words on the tip of my tongue can still
get lost or garbled in the attempt to utter them.*

*I'm falling less frequently, I'm happy to say — no doubt because
lurching experience has taught me to move around more cautiously —
but fumbling with buttons and zippers is not getting any easier. Jill
swallowed my pride for me and purchased a shirt and pants that close
with velcro! Now I can stand before friends and colleagues and rip
open my top to reveal a Superman t-shirt, like Clark Kent bursting
from a phone booth. Boy, is that a hoot!*

*I'm still dealing with constipation, even when I manage to drink the
eight glasses of water daily that also help limit urinary tract infections
(eight full glasses is not as easy to gulp down as you might think).
My hallucinations have stopped, although the novelty of seeing maps
everywhere I look is one quirk I've been sorry to see go. My admittedly
diminished cognitive skills aren't too bad most of the time, despite no
longer being able to read my own handwriting, and typos
multiply like fruit flies, no mater hwo fircely i concentarte.*

Back pains come and go, my voice will suddenly soften to a whisper, and words are becoming harder to find. I'm slower in my day-to-day comings and goings and I tire unexpectedly, but I'm finally on a regular exercise program, which helps. There may be some dementia in the offing, and I notice I'm acquiring a tendency to drool when my attention lapses…ooh, I can't wait for that to be a regular occurrence.

TMI? I guess it sounds like a lot to deal with, but I figure I can still choose to be happy. Happiness, after all, isn't just an outcome of circumstance or freedom from affliction — even though I wouldn't mind winning the lottery. For the most part, contentment is an inside job — an inner nexus of body, mind and soul that can be fed, ever and again, by the blessing of going outside, amid the solace of nature. Alongside that, I try to forgive whomever I need to forgive; accept everyone as they are, my rickety self included; and savor the moment, even the slightest breath of a saving moment.

I forget…have I mentioned the importance of nature? Bearing witness to the constancy of change, to nature's wax and wane, its coming and going, really is an affirmation of what it means to be alive. I know I'm not alone in struggling to be the best I can be; certainly nobody else can do this, not for any of us.

Oh — and have I said that you, too, should seek out nature as much as you can? The sun is high, the wind is fair… come out and join me in the open air.

Hey, that rhymes!

—ed

CPSIA information can be obtained
at www.ICGtesting.com
Printed in the USA
BVHW031052050820
585471BV00006B/20